The Story of One Word

When Life Doesn't Go the Way You Prayed

Clyde Teel

COFFEY
PRESS

COFFEY
PRESS

First Printing: 2019

ISBN: 978-1-09834-110-7

Clyde Teel
Sioux Falls, SD

Introduction

In the fall 2012 my wife Becky was diagnosed with pancreatic cancer. I want to share the depth of her struggle, the power of her faith, and the message of God's amazing grace through it all. It is not a story that ends how we all hoped it might, but I pray this story will challenge your thinking about who God is in our sorrow and pain. My goal is to bring a fresh word about His kingdom and a word of comfort to those who are hurting. Becky's journey was a long battle with a deadly disease. Her courage and faith will be evident as you read, and Becky would pray that God was glorified through all of it. I would like for you to get to know her…and Him.

I have chosen to write the stories we shared together during the cancer fight and at the same time talk about what I was learning in those long days. I am also going to include our family's social media posts during that journey. We used that forum to share with family and friends. I believe those posts will give you a deeper perspective and give you a look into our lives during the fight. I would like for you to get to know Becky and to see who she was during that time. My hope is that we can all learn something together about this tragic disease and the pain it causes families. I also pray you will see how God came to us in those profound moments of struggle.

I don't believe Becky (Mayer) Teel had an enemy in the world, and I mean that very sincerely. She treated everyone the same and anyone who knew her would tell you that was so. She was the last person deserving of such a thing to happen, but the first thing you learn with cancer is that life does not go how we plan or even how we choose. The best-lived life is no guarantee of the perfect outcome. The world is broken. When Becky found out she had cancer, life changed. We all changed, and that is the story I want to share. This is for everyone on a tough journey. I want to write about what I learned and what we went through. I want to give each one who reads these words a perspective on life and death. Where was God on Becky's journey?

Chapter I
The Perfect Life

Becky Mayer

I met Becky during our freshman year of high school. She was one of the "country kids" we "town kids" called them. She and her "country kid" classmates had been going to the small country schools around the city of Burke, SD. Burke is only a town of 700 so it is not exactly a metropolis. After those students Eighth Grade graduation, they would come into town to join the rest of us for high school.

I didn't notice her so much at first. It was a small class with only 43 students, so it wasn't like I was busy trying to get to know hundreds of people. I just didn't notice her. I guess she was just a part of the rest of us. The two of us sang a duet at the Junior/Senior Prom during our sophomore year, which as it turns out, would set the stage for a life of singing and music. We had no idea back then where any of this was going to go.

At some point during our junior year one of my good high school friends, John, told me there was a girl who had her eye on me. I thought he was crazy. What girl was going to be looking my way? The year before, as a sophomore, I was still the shortest kid in our class, and I could sing with all the sopranos. I had grown nearly seven inches the summer before my junior year, but I was still carrying that complex. John was pretty sure this one gal was watching me very closely. So, during choir one day I started watching Becky's eyes, and, sure enough, it did appear as though she had her "eye on me." Becky would later tell me that lots of girls thought I was cute, but just too short; as if I needed to be reminded.

After school one fine spring day John decided my slow, steady approach to this whole dating thing needed a little help, so he set a plan in motion to expedite the process. The plan was an elaborate maneuver to intercept Becky's car as she was driving home from school. After much fear and trembling on my part, John and I set off driving south of town in pursuit of the 1962 Fairlane filled with a half-dozen students and Becky in the driver's seat. We took great care not to be seen until the very last moment. His plan was to turn a mile early to the east and quickly (speeding at this point) get ahead of the Fairlane, then turn back south to

5

intercept her at the gravel intersection as she went to deliver her first passenger.

The plan was executed to near perfection. As we approached the crossroads, we looked, and there, just to the west of us coming over the hill was Becky. John pulled his car crossways in the middle of the road and stopped. She was trapped! I was trapped too! Now what? Do I say something? Do I wave? I had no plan, but I had nothing to fear as John was already out of the car flagging the Fairlane to a stop. He then proceeded to tell the entire carload of kids that it was *my* idea to come down there and see Becky. I just sat in the car and smiled.

The next day in school she stopped to talk to me and together we laughed about the silly plan that I assured her was not mine. We both blamed our good friend John for being so immature, but the relationship was now on a course that would not stop for over 4O years. We became high school sweethearts and the talk of the school. We were known as the "cute couple." We dated the through high school and four years later, on a hot August 4th at First United Methodist church in Burke, South Dakota, we were married.

....

"Growing Up" together

Becky was my girlfriend/evangelist. I was a "church kid," but much of my experience with God consisted of going to church with my family on Sunday mornings. I was a good kid and didn't get into a lot of trouble, but the idea of Jesus being my Savior was a thought that did not have a place in my life until I meant her. She was very cautious about how she would share with me. I knew she was very "religious," but I was okay with that. She had high standards and that told me she was someone I would like to get to know better. We talked often about God and faith, but I knew there was more going on in her than what was going on in me.

Becky's family was all about church. They did church it seemed to me nearly every day! There was always some church service we had to go to, but I really liked her so I was willing to go along with the whole thing. There was always singing in their home of the old gospel trios and quartets.

Becky's mom was always trying to get me to sing something in church. "Bring your guitar, Clyde," she would say, "and sing one of those good old country gospel songs." I would smile politely and decline the invitation. I would eventually give in to the request and sing for them. It was all a part of this grand plan to get me in their church, but I was on to their little scheme. I thought I was in complete control of how this was all going to play out. My confidence was based on my understanding of who God was and what I thought He expected. That idea was about to be challenged.

Becky grew up in a little country Pentecostal church right on the Nebraska/South Dakota border. I can still remember the first time I went there with her. I really enjoyed the singing and the all the enthusiasm. Those folks could sing! Pastor Vance was a passionate sort of fellow who always brought a good message, usually about end times. But when the prayer time came around, I was very uncomfortable. I wanted out of that place!

What in the world is wrong with these crazy people? Who does this sort of thing in church? What must God be thinking of us right now?

Becky and I would have lots of long conversations about what it meant to be spirit-filled. I was a little uncomfortable with all of that, but I didn't want to give up that pretty girl for a church. That seemed shallow to me.

To complicate things even more, I found out that her family was seriously struggling with my dating Becky. I wasn't a part of their church family. I hadn't grown up in that tradition and they were very concerned that their Becky was getting herself into a bad situation. It was not easy for a 17-year-old boy to be accused of corrupting a family's daughter. Becky and I would often talk about that problem.

My family was a bit concerned about Becky as well, or should I say concerned with how they perceived Becky's church. These church issues get around in a small community and her little country church on the border was not without a few *interesting* stories, none of which were true. People can get these false ideas about how churches should do things and then words get said that should not be said. Anyone who has ever grown up in a small town knows all too well how these stories can get around. So, Becky and I were both battling the odds. Still, we were convinced that our relationship was a good thing. It was now us trying to convince the rest of the world, and that was not the easiest challenge.

Becky would talk to me about deep God things. I was not without a fair understanding of such issues. I was a good student of these matters myself and I could hold my own in our discussions, but what I lacked was something much deeper and she knew it. So, she took me to an evangelist one evening in Platte, SD. The main reason I went was because the evangelist was a very fine guitar player and she knew how much I would enjoy that.

I was enjoying the concert and the fine guitar playing very much with my girlfriend. Then the guy started talking about Jesus and how He had come to give His life for my sins, and how all my good deeds amounted to nothing! I found myself somewhat reluctantly going forward during the invitation. Something or someone was compelling me to go. This was not about impressing Becky. It was something much more significant calling me and I knew it. That night my life changed. That evening I had what many would call a very dramatic conversion experience with God. It was a very powerful and one that I have never forgotten. The term "born again" has meaning to me.

I was not a bad person. I was depending on my deeds to get into heaven, and I discovered God needed my heart first. Becky knew. She had been praying for that. She was the one who brought me to Christ. It was my first encounter with God in that kind of way, and what it set in motion was a journey that Becky and I would share in the coming years. I had a deep sense that someday the ministry was calling me. I didn't know until years later that Becky had no sense of that calling. I guess we never really talked about that. There would be no way of knowing how that would all work out, but someone was calling me and I knew it.

That night changed a lot of things with her family toward me. They were still a bit cautious, but things were changing between us. My family began to see Becky as a great person and one that they could be proud of. We had both been blessed over the years with families that supported us. That is a gift we never took for granted.

After high school, Becky went to beauty school. (That's what people called it back in the day.) She said she picked that career because it was, in her words, the shortest period of time from being in school and starting a career. Little did she know, she would do that nearly her entire life. Becky could do hair! She was fast. Her skill and kind heart were a blessing to many customers throughout those years. It was good for us too. I can't imagine the dollars' worth of hair that fell on our kitchen floor. It would add up over 40 years.

At the same time, she was going to beauty school, I was going to school to be a music teacher. I was very excited about the plans we had made to do this life together. It seemed like everything was going just like we planned.

There were two little girls who came into our lives. Elizabeth was born during my junior year of college. We were trying to raise a child and finish school at the same time. That was a challenge. But when you are young, you don't think about things like that. At least we didn't. That's how life was. You just made the most of it. Abbie was born during my teaching years in Burke. They are four years apart in age and amazing young ladies. We could not be more proud!

Becky and I were very aware of how closely God was walking with us along the way. There were several moments, when faced with a new challenge, we would sit down and think it all through. There were a number of times we had to make hard decisions, but God would always show up at just the right time. It had built our confidence in how God worked things out in perfect ways. We could see His hand in so many ways. It was a faith-building journey for us.

We moved a couple of different times from O'Neill, Nebraska for my first teaching and then back to Burke, South Dakota to teach there as well. Becky started a little shop on Main Street to do that hairdressing business. "Duke & Duchess" she called it. It was a very successful business for her through all those years, and it came to be a very nice little shop in that small town. It was the place the girls and I would stop by after a day at school. We had purchased an old pop machine that still had glass bottles. And let me tell you, nothing is better than a cold, glass bottle of pop out of that machine after a hard day at school. We could sit in one of the swivel chairs in front of the mirrors and talk while Becky worked on someone's hair right next to us. It was a good life for us of just being a family in a small town. The years would rush by too quickly.

Before that move back to Burke, I had spent a couple of years working as a youth pastor in a church in O'Neill. This experience had really put the burn for ministry in my heart, but we made a decision that I would not pursue that direction until our girls were out of school. Those years of raising our girls and living our lives in that small town were very good years. I was having the time of my life teaching music and getting to go through school with my daughters. They were both deeply involved in music, and I was their music teacher. We did everything together. We traveled to music festivals, contests, concerts, and marching band competitions which then gave us all the same story to share. We could sit and not just tell each other about our day, but we could share the common experiences of our day. It was one of those rare gifts that we were given, and one that certainly gave us all a deep sense of wellness and security.

There was music in our family outside of school too. Our family traveled around and sang in the area for churches, special occasions, and community functions. Our little Christian band went through a number of changes throughout those years, depending on what style of music we were playing or what musicians were close by. It was a wonderful experience for us to share together. We did make a number of trips to Nashville in the mid-1980's to do some recording to try to determine if that was a direction we wanted to pursue. We decided *not* to go that way, and instead stick with the life that we fully believed God had called us to. We were going to get our daughters through school and then Becky and I would set out on our next journey, full time ministry.

This move would mean giving up "Duke & Duchess," and walking away from my teaching job, which after several years had grown into a significant music program for the community. The move was going to affect us and so many other people around us. This was going to be more than just a move; this was going to be a life change.

We were completely sold out to that decision and when Abbie graduated from high school in the spring of 1996, we began this new chapter in our lives. That summer we all prepared for the next step in our lives. Ministry is one of those vocations that involves the whole family. I realize that other jobs do as well, but in ministry we all know that the pastors and their families are "under the microscope" a bit. And whether real or perceived, it impacts everyone in some way. Even though our girls were grown up, we knew all too well each of us was going into something very new and very different. We were all excited for the change and ready for this new path on which God was taking us.

We found a nice little house in Sioux Falls, South Dakota close to the seminary. Through several good connections we were able to land five jobs between Becky and me. (I'm not kidding!) Our plan was to complete seminary in three years and move on to the next step. Becky and I were going to take on this new adventure with a great deal of enthusiasm. Becky was doing two jobs and anything else she could find to do. When you are excited about the new day you don't always see the potential problems, but even as I write out the plan now in black and white my mind is saying, *What were you thinking?* We thought it was the right way to do things. God had called us, and we are going to get this done.

....

The Seminary Years – The calling into Ministry

The next three years of our lives were going to be some of the best growing times of our journey, but Becky and I would be the first to tell you that our plan was flawed. It only took a few months of working this kind of routine and we were both spent. Physically, we were exhausted. Emotionally, we were drained. And spiritually, we were empty. Becky and I would often tell our friends that we had nearly lost each other and ourselves during that season of our lives. I loved school and the things I was learning. I enjoyed my professors and the students around me. It was so refreshing to wrestle with all the things I was learning and to have good friends to talk it all through, but when I would get home I was out of gas. Becky was an afterthought in some respects. I wasn't sitting in the beauty shop chair after school drinking a bottle of pop and sharing my day. Those days were gone. I had 20 private music students to take care of during my evenings and two other jobs to maintain as well. I was losing myself and her, one day at a time.

It was the most difficult time of our lives. Becky would agree. We managed by the grace of God and several long and bold talks with each other to get through those first two years. When my final year began I was already starting to get a handle on things. We were beginning to see the light at the end of the tunnel. The energy was coming back and we were making plans. I had an opportunity to do a little preaching in that final year in a small church in Sioux Falls that was actually looking for a pastor. They were in "search mode" and so I would fill the pulpit on the Sundays they had free. They were nice folks, but it was a denomination I had no affiliation with and wasn't really interested in. I was looking west. On my free weekends I would go back to Platte, South Dakota and preach in a little Baptist church on the north end of Main Street. It was the perfect little church. It was close to my hometown and a place with excellent hunting and fishing. Platte was like our second home and this was going to be perfect! We just knew it! God had brought us through a long difficult journey, but now the life we had both planned was coming together. Once again, God had done it. Oh sure, there were a few bumps, but now the horizon looked promising again.

However, God had another plan. The little church in Sioux Falls wasn't done with me quite yet. On a Sunday in late March, their search committee approached me and asked if I would consider putting my name on their list. I was grateful for their confidence, but shared with them just how much I didn't know about Reformed churches. My response to them was that I would "break it," but I told them Becky and I would pray about it.

Pray about it!

It is phrase we Christians use all the time and, for the most part, we really do mean what we say. But let's be honest, many times we already know what we are going to say. It is just a way for us to look spiritual. (Please don't be offended.) Becky and I actually did sit down and pray this through. When the answer came back we were both amazed, and even a bit shocked. We knew God was telling us to give up our dream job and stay in Sioux Falls. It was at some level so disappointing for us, but we had seen how God had worked in our lives all through the previous years. Why would we doubt Him now? We took the job and started our new journey in this new denomination. It would prove to be one of the best decisions of our lives. It has been 20 years now, and what an amazing work God has done in this place. We got to be a part of it. God is so good!

I went from being a music teacher to being a pastor. It has been a great life. Becky and I made that decision together a long time ago. We knew we would end up in this "business" of ministry. She was an amazing pastor's wife. She may not have been the typical pastor's wife because she didn't lead bible studies or play the organ every Sunday. Becky was just there for everything, and I mean everything. Her *way* was to be the consistent supporter, not only for me, but for so many others as well.

I would certainly never want anyone to think that our family had never experienced a disappointment or two, but our lives were very good over the course of those many years. It was almost as if everything we touched seemed to bring a great deal of happiness to us. We were a part of something very special. It wasn't that we set out with ambitious goals, but rather through making good choices (most of the time) and being very focused, all seemed to go well for us. It was like having the perfect life!

Chapter II
It's Cancer!

The Diagnosis

Stories like ours have a first day of cancer memory. Everyone's story has a few unique twists and turns as ours did. I have never forgotten that day. As I have visited with other people about their experiences, we all seem to share a common connection with the first moment you hear the "C-word." There is nothing you can do to prepare for what is coming. It is a disease that has no bias. Not your age, not your gender, not how rich or poor, it just comes at you. It takes you and your family to a new place.

In the winter of 2011 Becky had a terrible infection in her left shoulder that required an IV treatment of antibiotics for six weeks. It wasn't MRCA, but it was a close relative. She slept through nearly the entire month of February that year because the medications would make her so tired. It was another battle that poor girl faced in her life. I mention it here because we thought there was a connection to what was happening the following year with her being so tired all the time.

We thought it was probably just residual sleep needed after that infection battle, and for us, nothing to be that concerned about. Summer came that year and she still seemed to not be feeling the best. She was always so tired. She also was starting to have some issues with her upper tummy with too much extra air which led to a considerable amount of burping. It was embarrassing to her and aggravating for her to deal with, but still nothing of great concern. As we neared the end of the summer I suggested she set up a doctor's appointment and see what was going on. She had just seen the doctor in June for a full physical and everything seemed fine, but this, we both agreed, was just not right. The appointment was made. We needed to get to the bottom of this *small* anomaly. Maybe the doctor could prescribe some new meds and everything will be back to normal; at least that's what we thought.

We were having lunch at our house with our kids on Labor Day. It was a beautiful fall day, an absolutely perfect day. I had grilled burgers for lunch. (My burgers are quite a deal for our family.) We settled in for a lunch of burgers and beans. We were visiting about all kinds of things and having a great time around the table when our youngest daughter, Abbie, looked very intently at her mom and said, "Mom, are your eyes yellow?"

"You know," Becky said, "I wondered if I could see that yellow color a little this morning."

The whole family went into "fix it" mode and agreed that her eyes didn't look right. It was then we noticed that even her skin was tinted with that same yellow color. I knew it must be something liver related, but none of us were too upset. We quickly finished our meal together and called over to see if we could get in to Acute Care, which is our weekend medical center in Sioux Falls. Becky and I jumped into the car and headed over to see what was going on. I remember being a little concerned as we drove over, but not deeply worried. Becky was very calm. It is how she did anything like this, just a restful peace and never in a state of panic.

Calm. Every friend Becky has ever known would say this about her. There was nothing they would say to her that could ever change Becky's countenance. God was deep in this girl and we all knew it. I would often share with our church family that Becky was our "representative Pentecostal" in the group. I never meant that as a negative comment at all. She was a powerful witness of the presence of God in our church. She sat through every service, always in the front row, I mean *always*. People knew she was there. God was with her and it was evident.

The clinic was a short drive from our house so it didn't take long for us to get there. It was a holiday weekend and the clinic was not very busy; we got right in. They ran a couple of quick blood tests indicating an elevated liver count which explained the yellow color. Obviously those blood tests were not going to give us all the answers we needed so they set up an appointment to do a CT scan the following Wednesday morning. We left the clinic not all that anxious about what was going on. Looking back, we were a bit relieved knowing that we had at least found something. This elevated liver count might explain the fatigue too and probably the tummy gas as well. We felt like we were getting somewhere, and we were right on top of this new challenge.

Wednesday morning came and we went over to the scan center. We were completely unaware at this point in our journey that this scan business was going to become a regular part of her life for the next two years. We went right in and Becky drank that chalky drink, the contrast, and they took her back for the scan. It was all very professional. We were in, out, and home in just a couple of hours. Now we had to wait for the word to come back. We were a little concerned but certainly not overwhelmed with what might be coming. We don't get all worked up over things; that is not how we do life.

We had kept our girls informed this whole time. They seemed to be doing well with all this "yellow" business going on. However, we were all a little on edge because Becky had been through so much the year before. Those thoughts were in the back of our minds, but for the most part we were confident all of this would turn out just fine. We were thinking maybe the liver problem had something to do with all the meds she had taken from the year before and now we needed to take care of it.

Thursday morning the doctor's office called and said her results from the CT scan were ready, and it might be a good idea if Becky would "bring a family member with her." Everything changed!

I have dealt with hard things in people's lives many times before so I was very aware that when you hear, "bring a family member with you" this was serious. I was certain it was going to be bad news, but I was still positive. We are not a family that panics at every turn. We are positive people who are *motivated* by challenges. That is how we are wired. This was going to be one more opportunity to do what we always do. If God is for us, who can be against us? However, to be totally honest, down deep inside, I knew every heart was beating with an extra sense of urgency. Our minds were racing with questions. What could this be?

Friday came.

It was another beautiful fall day. I love the fall, and in South Dakota it can be one of the most amazing seasons to witness. You have these wonderful crisp mornings followed by warm afternoons of sunshine. The trees were just on the verge of changing colors and hunting season was coming. If you live in this state, it is the best time of year to be alive. That Friday morning was one of those days. We drove from our house to the clinic. We had not said much that morning getting ready because we had talked (I had talked) most of it through a dozen times the night before. Still, we had no idea what was ahead. I had made the mistake of doing a search on the internet for liver problems. I would highly suggest *not* to do that!

Arriving at the doctor's office we didn't have to wait long and we were ushered back to the waiting room. I remember it being the one on the left. There are just some details you never forget. We were sitting there in the room waiting for the doctor, but on this day waiting was very different. If you have never been in that place before, it is like being in another world. We were indeed *waiting*.

Doctor S. knocked on the door and came into the room. She was very professional in her manner as she entered the room. Dr. S. doesn't look like the kind of person who is going to give you bad news. She is very uplifting and pleasant, as if everything was just another day at the office. I suspected it wasn't. She greeted us as she crossed the room and sat down at her computer.

I was sitting in the chair next to her desk which gave me a good angle as I watched her opened the lab report on the computer. Becky had taken a seat on the exam table. Dr. S. opened up the file and started reading the results from the scan. I am sure she had already read through it, but in her professionalism, this is what you do. As she read along there were lots of large medical terms, each one missing their mark on my untrained medical mind. Then she stopped and turned toward Becky. I thought I could see tears in her eyes.

"Becky," she said, "I'm so sorry."

My heart stopped.

"Becky," she said, "You have a tumor in your pancreas. It's cancer."

I remember asking her, "How do you already know it is cancer?"

I wanted the world to stop for a moment. We all know about biopsies and tests. Surely we have to wait for those tests, right? You can't just come right out and say cancer!

"No. It's cancer. I'm so sorry," she said.

I slowly got up from my chair and walked over by the exam table and sat behind Becky. I listened as the doctor read through the report line by line. I listened as she described the size of the tumor and exactly where it was. Its location was such that it was pressing up against a bile duct closing the pathway in her liver, and that explained the yellow color. Somehow the yellow color didn't seem like such a problem now. The liver wasn't the problem anymore. It's cancer. It's *pancreatic cancer!*

Again, I'm not a doctor, but in my line of work I get to know a fair amount about diseases. This one is a killer, and I knew it. As I sat there, I was wrestling with two things on my mind. I was going back and forth on one hand trying to be the trained pastor who is good in these kinds of situations, and on the other hand being the husband/friend of the girl I have known for over 40 years. Without any awareness of it happening, my head had fallen against her shoulder and there were tears in my eyes. Words wouldn't come. I couldn't even form complete thoughts in my head. I was speechless, and for me to say such a thing is a big deal. I just sat there quietly. Becky was calm. Calm again.

Jesus, be near because this is really hard.

I don't really remember walking back through the clinic and out the front door, but I remember the sky. It was so blue that day and I remember thinking, how can it be so perfect and yet so imperfect at the same time? We walked across the parking lot to the car not saying a word to each other. We hadn't spoken a word to each other that whole time. I don't remember much of that conversation in the car either, but I remember her saying something like, "This is not about me. God has something more in mind. This is not about me."

We wondered how to tell the kids, and we talked about how that would go. All of our worlds were going to change now. It would be the same as picking up everything you own and moving to a new place to start all over again. The daily pace and regiment was all going to change in ways we couldn't know at that moment. There was a sadness inside like I have never felt and it would continue to overwhelm my heart at times. I am a preacher. I had walked through this kind of pain with others, but this was not others…this was Becky.

Let me tell you one of most difficult phone calls you will ever have to make in your life is sharing this kind of news with your kids. It was hard news for them, but at this point in the story we all had high expectations about how it would all go. Our attitude was to do this long journey one day at a time. We believed God was going to do some amazing things and we didn't want to miss any of them. We were confident that lives were going to be touched, ours too .

Sharing The News

I suppose there is really no easy way to share news like this. You just get people on the phone and say it straight out.

We started calling folks. I don't remember how that went. I just remember being drained by it all.

The girls and I also decided to use social media as a means of sharing Becky's story. Social media was a relatively new thing for me at the time, but I knew it could be a valuable tool in the ministry of a church and could be especially effective for a certain age demographic. Posting our news would be a way for us to keep everyone up to speed with what was going on with Becky so we wouldn't have to tell the story over and over to each person we saw. As it turned out, that decision was one of the best things we could have done. I know many people have used tools like online health journals to connect to those who want to know, but we used the social media format.

Then there was our church family. They are one of the reasons I wrote this book. I am a pastor of a wonderful community of people. I am an alive, spirit-filled, evangelistic, Jesus is Lord kind of preacher. Becky and I had poured our lives into this church. We loved these people, and over the course of 15 years we had seen God build this amazing community of believers into one of the most spiritually healthy churches we could ever have hoped to be a part of.

As a church we had been growing steadily. Community was a 50-year-old church plant that had outgrown the original building. With the passion of these people and their vision we had relocated to the east side of town only a couple of years earlier. The new building was built in the middle of cornfield. (It really was in the middle of a cornfield.) It is an amazing place of grace! We had only been in the building for three years, but because of our growing number of young families and their children, we had to add on. I was the senior pastor of this great church and on the upcoming Sunday, now only one day away, we were going to start a drive to raise the funds to build a new education wing. Our family was going through this crazy mess and the church could not be doing better. Everyone at church was excited. It was "Kickoff Sunday." My thoughts were so conflicted.

Really God? This Sunday? This is your perfect timing? I am supposed to get up in front and talk about a building? Will they even hear one word I have to say when I tell them this news?

Becky and I decided right from the beginning that we were going to live every moment of this in front of our church family. We weren't looking to get their sympathy or highlight our struggle, but we wanted to show them how God was going to work through it all. We made the decision not to hide any of it. We believed this would become an opportunity to grow us all deeper. It was an important time in the life of the church and we understood that, but hiding this was not going to be an option. God was going to get us through!

That Sunday church started like any other Sunday. Some of the people arriving that morning already knew because the word gets out, but most of those coming through the doors did not know. I do three services on Sunday mornings and as we worked through the morning it became more and more difficult to keep my emotions together. I remember specifically at the 9am service when I announced the news of Becky's cancer, there was an audible gasp from our friends as they listened. It was a sad day. Becky sat in her usual place at all three services. It was hard for her to watch and hear the people hurting. She would later tell me it was one of the saddest days of her life.

I typically work far ahead in my sermon preparation. I will take time several months before a sermon series to work up an outline for each of the upcoming messages. This had become a part of what people expect of me. It had become a faith-building resource for all of us. It was amazing to see how those messages would line up with lives and situations. It's an amazing "God Thing!" My reasoning for working so far ahead is simple. I believe God already knows what is coming. God is ahead of us. Our regular church attenders knew this was who I am, but on this day, I am sure many of them were wondering if I was going ahead with what I had prepared in advance.

On this Sunday we have "cancer" going on. How will that fit?

You can go listen because all the messages are online. If you do, you will discover I didn't change one single idea. The words spoken that day were exactly what we needed to hear. God was still in control. I thought I was going to be doing a series about a new building and a new vision, but the words were telling us it was not about a building; it was about a God who can do amazing things "in, around, and through us." The campaign was off and running and we were off and running too. Cancer was now our life. How would these two paths travel together? All we could see was God getting bigger. We were going to win! This was going to make us all deeper, stronger, and more excited for what God was going to do.

My first social media post:

> *To all our friends*
>
> *Becky has been diagnosed with pancreatic cancer. We don't have every detail yet, but we know there is a tough journey ahead of us. People have already been amazing...and God is getting bigger.*

....

Oncology

Our battle started with the first procedure, which was to get a stent put into the bile duct of the liver so we could relieve that pressure and allow the bile to flow once again. This would clear up the not so lovely yellow color from her skin and eyes. The surgeon was also going to try to get a biopsy of the tumor to confirm what we had been told. At this point I was still holding out hope that maybe that crazy little tumor would turn out *not* to be cancer.

The surgery was an outpatient procedure, so only one day and we would be home. It would be the first of many days walking through hospitals and clinics for us, but we were positive this was going to work in our favor. Pancreatic cancer is often found too late. It typically grows in a place that is hidden away deep in our core and by the time it is found it has usually progressed to dangerous levels.

However, we had been told that because her tumor happened to grow right against a bile duct maybe it was kind of a first miracle. We had found the cancer in its early stage. That yellow color was just like a giant red (in this case yellow) flag telling us that a problem was occurring. From the very beginning we had this confidence that God was working ahead of us. After all, how many good folks were praying by now? Hundreds of people were already offering prayers and sharing about how they were supporting us in this new day. We could see God's hand already at work, and this was looking like just another piece that was coming together in our "favor."

The stent surgery went well and as Becky was recovering back in the room. The surgeon spoke with me briefly about the procedure. He said the stent was placed without much trouble, and we could expect the color to change very soon. I asked about the biopsy, and he said he tried several times to hit the target. He said he was certain he was "right in there" a couple of times. Then he said those samples were negative.

I thought, *Negative? You mean not cancer?* He said he could not be certain he was on target, but I didn't hear much of that. When you are looking for good news you grab anything that comes along. I was cautious, but I was thinking maybe we had dodged a bullet. Looking back now I think we were all just a bit too overly optimistic, but it was hopeful news. We let people know there was a chance that maybe it was not cancer. This was some potential good news. However, what we could not see was a journey that was going to be filled with many ups and downs and would prove to be mentally draining in the coming weeks and months.

The next meeting was with Dr. M., our oncologist. We were hoping he could shed a little light on all these findings. Dr. M. is someone Becky knew only too well. She had battled through breast cancer in 2000. That's right. This was her second run in this cancer race.

Becky's breast cancer is another story to tell about our journey together. I was just finishing my seminary degree to be pastor in 1999. Graduation was a few days away when we got that news that Becky had breast cancer.

I remember thinking,

> *We have given up everything to do this church business. Now this? God, how can this be your plan?*

Becky stayed the course and did everything with such grace and confidence. She won. God was there and we learned then that even when we can't see why, God is still working. It was a victory. Another connection was during that breast cancer battle the same church folks walked through it with her. As mentioned earlier, we had taken a job at this Reformed church in Sioux Falls even though we really wanted to go to Platte, but we were so convinced that God was directing our steps. He had been with us through so many things and in so many ways. We had seen Him work.

I hope you are reading through these pages with your focus on the "plan." The timing of this story at every turn is going to grab your attention before we are through. There was never a doubt through any of this that God was involved, but it is not the way any of us would ever design it. There is much more I will say about all this later. For now let me say that we were in for the ride of our lives and, at this point, we were just getting started.

The church prayed over her in 1999 to heal that cancer, and they had supported us the whole time. We stayed positive that whole time. After some nasty radiation treatments, Becky's cancer was under control. The point is that she had been on this cancer path before and she had won. God was on the throne in '99. We knew the power of prayer and the amazing gifts that God had for us. We were not defeated! We were ready to talk to Dr. M. because "he will know what to do."

Becky knew right where to go for this appointment. She had visited this place many times long before this day. Every year she would go in for her annual check-up which by now, she had been doing for years. It was a familiar place to her, but our meeting that day was going to change our lives forever. We didn't know what was ahead of us. We walked through the doors of the clinic. Immediately people were saying hello to Becky. It felt good to me. I loved those people from that very first meeting and I thought, *It is going to be okay. We have caught this crazy thing early. We can do it!*

Once again we were escorted into one of those small rooms. And once again we were waiting. I don't remember any of the conversation Becky and I had while we waited. I remember looking at photos on the walls of the room. They were old pictures of graduating Navy men and women from back in what appeared to be the second World War. It brought a sense of connection to the past and I liked that feeling.

Dr. M. came in and said hi to Becky. It was just like one old friend to another. He sat down to look over the chart. Dr. M. is an interesting man, always wearing his signature bow tie. A tall sort of fellow who really *does* look like someone who does what he does. I'm not trying to stereotype the characters in this story. The point I'm trying to make is there is a special kind of comfort in *knowing* these doctors and having confidence in who they are and what they do. It's all about looking for a place to stand. When you are doing battle with this kind of enemy, those small things matter. Every person and every situation has meaning for you. You are looking for any kind of foundation when the ground beneath you is constantly shifting.

Dr. M. is a let's-get-to-the-point kind of guy. He never beats around the bush, and I remember him saying, "Okay, we need to get this thing out of there."

I knew that meant surgery but first I wanted to know, "Is this cancer? Do we know for sure what it is? We are after all holding out a glimmer of hope that maybe this isn't the big 'C-word.'"

He replied back in his calm demeanor, "It needs to come out."

"But what about the biopsy?" I asked.

"He might have missed it." Dr. M. went on to explain the complexities of trying to hit that three-dimensional target with a two-dimensional picture on a screen. With that one clarifying statement we were back to the reality we had been hoping to avoid, but I still wondered if it was cancer. I was not willing to give in on this one. I have looked back on all that now realizing that no doubt there were other indicators pointing the doctors in the direction of cancer. They do this all the time, but for me it was all new. You discover as you go along these new journeys that there is so much to learn and experience. At some point you just have to trust someone. That is not always easy.

The first matter of business was the simple fact that the tumor had to come out. So Dr. M. started firing questions, "Where do you want to do the surgery? Do you know a surgeon? Do you want to do it in Sioux Falls?"

We had been doing our homework on this. We knew of a thing called the Whipple Surgery. We had several doctor friends who had explained this to us in great detail, much of which we did not understand. Most of them agreed that if it was their loved one, they would go where they do many of these procedures every week, the Mayo Clinic in Rochester, Minnesota. Becky was ready for his question. "I think we would like to go to Mayo," she said.

"I think we would like to go to Mayo," she said.

Dr. M fired right back, "I'll make the appointment. We need to get this done as soon as possible."

And just like that we were off and running. I don't remember much of what we said that day after we left the clinic. I know what I was feeling, fear and sadness. I know we would all like to think that in those tough moments our faith, and, in my case, my professional training will rush in and take over, but it is not as simple as you might think.

There are deep moments of fear. There are moments when your heart is beating so hard that you are aware of literally every tick, moments that pull at your very soul and they hurt. It was during those moments, and only then, that I would sense a comfort which began to come over me. It wasn't sudden. It was slow but evident. I asked Becky so many times during her journey how she was doing. I wanted to know what it is like to be where she was. Her words were always calm. Sometimes there would be tears because she did not want to be in that place, but she was certain there was a reason behind all of it. She was always confident that it would *not* take her life.

At this point we were getting all kinds of encouragement. People were sharing stories of family members who had gone through the surgery and made it. We had people we didn't even know calling to give words of hope. Cards were pouring in all the time. People wanted to know what was happening and what was next. We discovered that Becky's story was getting out. It was the story of this pastor's wife going through this awful thing. We were talking about it in church and being real with our people. The battle was on, and we were going to win! We didn't hide any of it from our church. If it hurt; I said it. If it made us sad; we said it!

I discovered that people wanted to hear the reality. They wanted to know what it was like. That's what they wanted to hear. The journey began to take on a life of its own. Becky was becoming an amazing story of the power of God in the midst of struggle. It became a life-giving story of hope to people who were in those tough places. It seemed like the whole thing had a purpose and that purpose was growing every day. I would get ready to speak on Sundays and Becky would remind me nearly every time, "*Now* you have something to say."

At first, I didn't know if I liked that so much.

We would laugh together about it, but I began to understand what she meant. As the time would pass her words would take on a whole new meaning; she never once wavered from that position, not even on the most difficult days. Her word to me was always, "If you stop now in the face of this disease, what does that say about this amazing God we have in us? Do we give up now when there is so much to say?" she would ask.

It was a powerful testimony she was carrying deep inside. Many of our friends had her say that directly to them. There was something moving in her and everyone close to her knew it.

It was a tough time to be sure. This was not easy. Everything was moving so fast. You wait for the diagnosis and test results which seems to take forever, and then suddenly the world is turned upside down. You are racing along at breakneck speed to the next appointment and to the next place. Days seem to run together and in a matter of moments you are being carted off by this speeding train to the next destination.

Can we just slow it all down for a bit?
I need time to think it through.
Are we doing the right thing?

There is no training manual. I didn't take this class in school. Not even with my seminary training could I find a formula. I just remember the words of one of my amazing seminary professors who would say to us, "The only way out...is through."

"The only way out... is through."

Those words were ringing in my weary ears. I guess we do another day Becky. I don't like this one bit. Struggle is hard, and don't let anyone tell you differently. And then in the middle of my pain something would happen. Slowly at first, but I would notice my heart settling. God was there again.

I haven't said much about our girls. They too were writing to friends and posting their thoughts on social media. This was their mom and their hearts at times were breaking. Still as they wrote it down you could tell something was working deep in their lives as well. We were all going through this. I know there are lots of children watching a mom or dad go through things that are scary. I think Liz and Abbie's perspectives are vital in this journey. There will be more to follow, but here is what they were saying at this point.

Liz wrote:

> *Alright, friends... As many of you already know, my Mom Becky Teel has been diagnosed with what doctors are sure is Pancreatic Cancer. This morning, she will go in for a biopsy to confirm that diagnosis as well as find out what kind of cancer we will be fighting (the results probably won't be in until Monday). We already see God's hand all over this. For instance, the cancer was caught very early (it's only about 2 cm) due to other symptoms that had nothing to do with her pancreas. We know this road will be long and difficult, but we know Who is traveling it with us. We are not alone! And we are not without hope! "We are hard pressed on every side, but not crushed; perplexed, but not in despair; persecuted, but not abandoned; struck down, but not destroyed." - 2 Cor. 4:8-9. Thank you so much for your outpouring of encouraging words and prayers. We are so thankful for you!*

> *Here's a little more info on my Mom...*
> *Today Mom and Dad met with their oncologist. The lab results were not done, so we still don't know whether or not this is cancer. However, that information doesn't really matter at this point because the tumor must come out, and the sooner, the better.*
> *They have decided to do this big surgery at the Mayo Clinic. We are hoping Mom and Dad will be contacted by Mayo within the week to make an appointment for preliminary tests in order to have the surgery. (Mayo will probably do their own biopsy there.) Recovery for this surgery will probably be 7-10 days in the hospital if everything goes well. Once the tumor is out, and doctors have had the chance to thoroughly test it, we'll meet with the oncologist to see what further treatment is necessary (if any). We are encouraged and ready to get on with getting this thing out of her. :) God continues to move in powerful ways. We absolutely feel your prayers and love, dear friends! As Dad said on Sunday, God's grace washes over and over us to give us whatever we need for each day. God is so big, and getting bigger... :)*

> *We'll keep posting more as we know more. Thank you, thank you, thank you for your prayers!*

Abbie wrote:

> *Becky Teel speed update: She and Dad met with the oncologist...no lab results yet...tumor needs to come out no matter what...not doing a second biopsy in Sioux Falls...waiting for a call this week from Mayo to schedule tests and surgery (hopefully in the next couple of weeks)...surgery recovery is 7-10 days in hospital (more outside of the hospital, of course)...we'll know more once they have the tumor outside of her body and can really take a look...Mom and Dad were very encouraged by the oncology visit (as encouraged as they can be when looking at the tough road ahead)...God is very near.*
>
> *There is a saying that "God doesn't give you more than you can handle." I think I disagree with that. I think God gives us more than we can handle, so HE can step in and take over for us. That's what we continue to experience with Him. Believe me, your prayers are being heard and felt. Thank you! This is definitely not about Mom or our family...It's about God's power, grace and glory.*

Becky's first words:

> *It felt soooo good to be in church this morning and see all of my community family and feel the presence of God. Thank you everyone for all the prayers that have gone up on my behalf!! I can definitely feel them holding me close. Please keep them coming as Clyde and I head for Mayo tomorrow. I know I am in God's arms and His timing is perfect!! One step at a time..........*

Chapter III
The Next Battle

The First Visit to Mayo

I had never been to the Mayo Clinic. I had heard amazing things about the place, but I was about to find out for myself. This trip was going to be, once again, nothing we could have ever planned for. The train ride was about to pick up speed.

It is about a four-hour drive to Rochester, Minnesota from Sioux Falls. It was another one of those perfect fall days. It was October now and the leaves were changing. It was a beautiful time to be on the road, but to be honest, none of that seemed to make much difference to us. We talked about all kinds of things, but mostly about this cancer thing and what might happen.

We were going for a meeting with the doctors. We thought we were going to be doing a couple of tests, a quick visit, set up a time for surgery, and then come home to share the news. That was the plan. That was *our* plan. I didn't check with the conductor of that fast-moving train. We said goodbye to our kids and drove off for another round of whatever was ahead.

We arrived there in the evening and checked into our hotel room for the night. Our appointments were all set for the next day. I was hoping we could find our way around this new place because that is always a bit intimidating for me, navigating new turf. I suppose it is a little of that "small town" in me that wants to be able to know the exact layout of everything.

We had a nice dinner that evening together. I don't remember much of our conversation, but those were special times. My mind was constantly moving. I don't remember being restless, just hurting.

Becky was always able to sleep at night. She could sleep through any kind of stress. When it came time to lie down for the night, she could do that with no problem. Her sense of calm was evident that evening. It was as if nothing new was coming. I'm sure there was some uneasiness deep inside, but I couldn't see it and I knew her better than anyone. The morning would soon come.

It was Tuesday morning and time to get going. I remember driving over to the building and finding the parking ramp. We turned in and got a great parking spot. I'm not really that competitive, but finding a good spot close always seems like I've accomplished some great feat of driving skill. Becky wasn't that impressed, but she was always in that supportive frame of mind. We were there. A short walk to the elevator in the parking ramp, down the elevator to the lower deck, a short walk under the street into the clinic, out into this amazing rotunda of marble walls and floor. It was the Mayo clinic.

There were all these people. Obviously, there were doctors and workers, but there were all these *wounded ones*. There were wheelchairs bustling around and people looking at their maps. It seemed as though everyone was going some place quickly.

We stopped to ask for directions at the front desk and then off we went down the long hallway. There was a grand piano there and a musician playing something; it might have been an old hymn. We walked down to the elevator and up to our floor. We had to do a couple of tests first and then go over to another part of the clinic to meet for the first time with our surgeon. We checked in at the front desk where we met this very funny gal. She made us feel very at home, gave us our little buzzer, and told us to have a seat.

Waiting again.

We were early of course. That's one of our family things. We are not just on-time people. We are early arrivers. It is something our girls have come to understand about their dad. Whatever time I say, I really mean 15 minutes before that. Becky knew as well and she had just come to adjust her life that way without ever saying a single word about it. We are a family who does things together. We know each other and understand each other. It's our normal.

Normal. Our normal was being invaded. A new normal was slowly starting to take over. It was happening without our awareness. For those who go through these long journeys, you know all too well what I am saying. A new "normal" was coming. Maybe it was already there and we just didn't know it. There were times during the battle that I would have given anything to have nothing going on. That day was not going to be that particular Tuesday!

Our little buzzer started going off and we heard the nurse call, "Becky Teel?"

We were taken back to one of those small rooms again and we waited there for a few minutes. There was a gentle knock on the door, and in walked a young lady who kindly introduced herself and sat down at the desk. She began to make her way through the large pile of paperwork we had brought with us. It was dozens of pages of medical reports and scan results. She was paging along with amazing speed and would stop occasionally to ask a clarifying question.

I would tell people later that I think I might have been talking to one of the smartest people I had ever met. She could look at a page for only a moment and then instantly be able to share the content as if she had read it over and over a dozen times. It was impressive. "We aren't in Kansas anymore, Toto." No offense meant to my friends in Topeka, but I think you understand the point. These are highly skilled/trained medical people who do their jobs with wonderful precision. The sheer volume of patients dealing with similar issues has made these folks experts in their fields. She stopped and gave us the preliminary findings and suggestions of what to do next. It all made perfect sense to us, and after a couple of other questions for us, she was finished. "The doctor will be in shortly."

> "The doctor will be in shortly."

Dr F. came in. We didn't know at the time, but he was one of the finest surgeons in the world. He was an expert at the Whipple procedure. He too looked over the information and the charts we had brought with us and turned to ask if we might be willing to stay another day or two so they could do some more detailed scans. We agreed to do that. We had come to the Mayo Clinic get something done and we were willing to do whatever it would take. He assured us they would do everything possible for us, but he also reminded us of the seriousness of what we were dealing with. We didn't need to be reminded.

When he left, another nurse came in and told us how fortunate we were to have Dr. F. She shared with us that he was one of the best in the world in this field. There it was again. God had gone ahead of us. We didn't know any surgeons. We just took the first one available and it turned out to be Dr. F. God was working and we knew it! You begin to gain such a sense of confidence because you are seeing things come together. You are overwhelmed with knowing there are hundreds of people praying for things to go just like this, and when it happens you just want to shout! Go God Go!

I wonder how many times in our lives God goes ahead of us taking care of details? I am sure it happens much more than we are even aware. How many dozens of perfect encounters are set in motion long before we ever know? I know theologically speaking, it is all about God's work and His hand in everything around us. To us living in the moment it is not always that evident. But if you are looking, God does seem to be everywhere. This journey was already beginning to show us just how amazingly involved God was in all the pieces of our lives. These "God Things" as I like to refer to them, are going to keep coming at us. God really was there at every turn.

As this story continues to unfold I hope you will see God too. There will be things that will amaze you. You may read certain points of this story and question the truth of it. But let me assure you that no embellishment is needed. Becky's journey was lived out in front of hundreds of people who were all aware of each detail. God was amazing!

We left the clinic knowing we needed to get another place to stay for the night. So we went for a drive. We looked for another place to stay, something away from everything. We found a nice hotel on the edge of town with a small lake on the north side. There was even a walking path. It was perfect. We got our room and settled in for the evening. It had been a long day.

The next day we had to run over to the clinic for another scan which didn't take long, and we were finished by noon. Now what? There was nothing to do until the next day. I hadn't brought a single thing to fill all this time. I did have my computer so I could do my church work, but I didn't think to bring my guitar. I'm a musician! I find great comfort and solace in the time I have with playing my instruments. I decided to stop at one of the local pawn shops in Rochester and see what they had. The search for a guitar became an exciting adventure. It was something out of the ordinary in this new normal. I found a guitar in the very first pawn shop and I made an offer. We were having some fun. It felt like our life was back again. It was as if we were getting something back that we had lost. We both affectionately called my new purchase "The Cancer Guitar." I had a way to fill some of the long hours that were ahead. I would play guitar, and Becky would read. It was like being home again.

The following day was Wednesday and we went back to the clinic for a visit with our doctor again. We knew we would get some information that would move things along.

Things were going to start happening now. It felt good to be getting somewhere, and we were confident that this was going to work out. We knew the ropes now. We knew the building. We can do this! God had been working overtime for us it seemed and hundreds of people were praying. *God is getting bigger!*

God is getting bigger!

Doctor F. told us the tests all looked favorable for surgery. Up until that point we hadn't really concerned ourselves with the possibility that they couldn't do it. He informed us that until he actually "got in there" he couldn't be sure he could proceed. I knew all too well if she couldn't have the surgery the chances of her living were very small. This was a major hurdle and one we hadn't thought about until that moment. I just kept thinking of all the things that had worked out for all of this.

It looked good, right? We had caught it early because of the plugged bile duct that just "happened" to get blocked because the tumor was *perfectly* located to give us that warning, right? God was working ahead of us again, right?

Then he turned to Becky and said, "I can do it Friday."

"Friday?" I asked, "You mean *this* Friday?"

Once again my mind was racing: I thought we were going to make an appointment and go home. I mean, you have to get ready for a thing like this. We have all kinds of things coming up this week. Friday?

We talked back and forth with him and he informed us he would be leaving that weekend to go teach a class overseas, and he wouldn't be back for two weeks. He stressed to us that we really need to get this done, and if he was going to do it, it had to be now. Dr. F. told us he would stop back for our decision in a moment. His nurse told us to talk it all through. She said they would make some other rounds and be back for our decision. She ended with, "You really need to do this. He's the best there is!"

I know...but Friday?

We were now alone in that room again. The fast-moving train was gaining speed again. We could clearly see how God had been so involved up to this point, *But really, God? How can this be the right timing? It's coming at us so fast. Why can't we have time to prepare? Isn't taking time always a better plan in the grand scheme of things?*

We were learning that trusting in God means to trust in His timing too. It really does mean to lean on His, and not our own, understanding or preparation. That is a tough lesson to learn when you are a planner. I am good at preparing for things, but this week of all weeks! So why was this week so special?

This question will open up another part of Becky's story I mentioned earlier. It is one of the most significant parts of her life and our lives as a family. It has been a kind of glue that has bonded Becky and I together since we met nearly 40 years ago. It is something our family does and we love it. Music.

If you will recall Becky had grown up in a family that sang all the time. Her sisters sang in church nearly every week. Her mom, Betty, was always working in the church on the music end of things. It was their music that opened my eyes to a God who is not dead. It was through the music.

My family was also a musical family. My dad and his brothers played music as young boys on the farm during the Dirty Thirties. My grandpa would go around to farm sales and buy instruments for the boys to play. My grandpa wasn't a musician, but he wanted those boys to learn to play. They would have school dances in the old country school on the Whetstone Creek and invite all the neighbors. It was a way to raise the spirits of people during a hard time. My dad grew up listening to the Grand Ole Opry on the neighbor's radio. I have bluegrass roots in my blood. I grew up with music.

Our lives were wonderfully woven together by this gift we got to share. Becky wanted to learn to play guitar when we first were married, but we learned that having a husband try to teach his wife how to play guitar can lead to some not so healthy exchanges. She got very frustrated with all my instruction and gave up rather quickly. However, her secret ambition was to play bass. Years later as I was teaching some of our church folks a basic guitar class, she asked if she could come to the class and learn bass with some of the other bass players.

"Really? The Bass? Okay, but you're on your own. You'll be just another student; not my wife!"

She smiled, "Okay."

She did it, and she was very good. She started playing in our family band and played in the contemporary praise band in church as well. She loved it! We all did! I could go on and on, but I won't. I just want to paint this part of the story with an understanding of just how important these things can be for a family. Our daughter, Abbie, gave her mom and I a plaque for Christmas one year that still hangs in the kitchen with the words, "A family that plays together, stays together." For us and our family-life together, it was *soul deep*.

> "A family that plays together, stays together."

This takes me to why that next week was so important. We had contracted to have one of our favorite bluegrass bands come to our church, and we were going to get to open for them. Ricky Skaggs was coming to *our* church. It was a big deal to us. We had met him before, and he had agreed to come back and do a concert in the church as a unique outreach event. Becky was looking forward to being a part of that night, and now that would be gone. It might seem that playing a concert is a rather insignificant thing when compared to the bigger things we were dealing with at that moment, but when you are in the midst of these battles you hold on to anything that brings joy. You don't throw small things to the side as if they don't matter, because they do.

We knew what to do. We knew the right thing to do. We didn't need a lecture from anyone. We were both disappointed, but we had to do the surgery on Friday. We knew it from the moment he said it.

We drove back the hotel both a little stunned by the hour we had just shared together. We had no idea what the Whipple was going to be like. You can read all about it, but nothing can really prepare you for what is ahead. There is no way to know. Life has those moments when the only way to really understand something is to step into it. Do not misunderstand me, preparing and learning are valuable tools in life's tool belt, but it is a false sense of security. Knowing with your mind is not the same as what the experience will teach you. The experience will be its own teacher. I would learn in the coming days what it means to "experience" life. Right now our focus was getting this surgery done.

Becky called some friends and family that night from the room. She read her book too. She seemed so calm and so at peace with all this craziness that was surrounding her. We talked about our week and we talked about what the next day might be like. She said she just wanted this next part to be done and get on the other side of surgery, and then in a few weeks things will be different. I played my "cancer guitar" a little and then we both fell asleep. Morning would come.

....

The Whipple

I had never heard of this surgery until Becky's cancer, but it was a new word that showed up almost immediately after the diagnosis. I had now learned it was one of the most complex surgeries in the world. It was even more complicated (I was stunned to learn) than open-heart surgery. The Whipple is a surgery in which a large, nearly 18 inch incision, is made laterally across the midsection of your upper torso as the surgeon follows your rib line. This curved incision creates a flap of skin that is opened up to reveal your entire upper digestive track. The surgeon begins to work through all these organs until they finally reach the pancreas lying just below the liver. Your pancreas is at the very core of your body.

I didn't mean to make you queasy with all those details, but you need to understand what is involved with this procedure to fully appreciate the level of skill it takes to make a successful resection of this tumor and the amount of healing time it takes before things begin to come back to life. We were told that all the upper "plumbing" of your entire digestive system is being "unplugged." Some of it will be removed and then every system has to be all hooked up again. One by one all those systems have to come back "on line." This is going to take an amazing bit of surgical precision to bring about a successful outcome. Becky was going to be in surgery for nearly eight hours or longer, depending on all kinds of possible variables. All of that needs to be done just to get at this naughty little tumor in that pancreas. My job will be to wait…again.

Jesus be near because this is going to be hard.

We arrived very early that morning at St. Mary's hospital in Rochester for our day. It was a cold morning as we pulled up to the front doors. I let Becky out and drove down into the underground parking ramp below the hospital. I quickly found a spot and hit the elevators to get up to the main floor. She was waiting there in the hallway along with dozens of other people all waiting in line for the morning's various procedures. I was surprised by the number of people gathered there that morning. We took our place in one of the long lines to check in. I don't remember saying much as we were standing there, but I do remember thinking about how fast things had happened.

We had come to Mayo to get some direction. We thought there would be some tests and some discussion about scheduling. We thought that might take a few days to workout. We thought we would have time to go home and talk to our kids...you know...pray about it, but here we are in this line. Surgery is going to happen in just a few minutes. You are trying to gather yourself up and be strong, but it is all coming at you so fast. You are quickly discovering that what you are really doing is reacting to the next situation or circumstance. Certainly, there is some degree of planning and preparation, but it is more than your heart can actually take in.

You look around and you also realize you are not alone in your struggle. There were others in the line with us. I'm sure not every case was as complicated or life-threatening as ours, but each of them had a story and everyone in that line had friends and families who were waiting with them somewhere. We were all there together and our minds were all very busy that morning.

We waited in line only a few minutes as it moved very quickly. The check-in procedure was a well-oiled machine. When we arrived at the front of the line we gave the young lady our info and she gave us our packet and asked us to find seat in this large waiting room. She assured us someone would be calling us very soon.

We found a couple of chairs and sat down, once again, waiting. As we sat there, both of us noticed a young couple with small children sitting not too far from us. We could tell by their actions that something had them very concerned. The young lady was crying. The husband was doing his best to console her and manage the two small children at the same time. One of the nurses stepped into the room and called out a name. It was her. She got up, went over and hugged both kids, gave him a little kiss, and walked away. We wondered, what that was going to be? We talked about that after she left. We felt bad for them. Here they are just starting out their lives and they were in this place now. It gave us pause. We have had a good life up this point. This new challenge was ahead of us, but lots of people were going through hard things. We were not the only ones.

"Becky Teel?" the nurse said.

It was our turn. When we stood up I thought for a brief second if people were looking at us and wondering why we were there? Did their hearts go out to us? Did they see something that captured their attention about why we were there? Maybe it was just my mind working too hard. I don't know.

We got up and went with the attendant who asked Becky if she wanted a wheel chair because it was going to be a long walk. She answered that she thought that might be nice, so he quickly found one and off we went down a long series of hallways and elevators. This maze of pathways seems to be the rule of thumb for so many hospitals these days. They are continually building on new wings and remodeling old ones. St. Mary's hospital has been there for years. You can see it is an older building, but very well maintained. We arrived at the "get ready" room for our pre-surgical consultation. A nurse was waiting for us when we arrived. I'm sure for her this was all in a day's work. Another day. So routine in many ways, but for us it was a whole new experience. The very first thing Becky had to do was change into one of those lovely hospital robes, and then she took a seat on this rather large high chair sitting in the corner. The nurse spoke, "Becky, your full name and birth date please."

Becky quickly answered, "Becky Teel. Six, eighteen, fifty-three."

"Becky Teel. Six, eighteen, fifty-three."

I have no idea how many times along the journey I had heard that question and listened to that answer. Hundreds I'm sure! For any of you reading who have been in those places, you will know exactly how this routine looks and sounds. I never heard Becky complain about having to give that information, even though she did it over and over. Those moments become reminders of a time and a place. I have never forgotten how she said that phrase. She said it nearly the same way every time, even when she was so weak and tired. It would come out with the same word rhythm and inflection.

"Becky Teel." (Accent "Teel" just a little.) "Six, eighteen, fifty-three." (The fifty-three would go down in pitch and end softly.) Every time it would come out that way. It may sound a little crazy, but the sound of those words has been imprinted in my mind. I think those moments stick with us because there are stories and memories attached to them. Each day we are adding another layer to those stories.

Becky was being prepared for surgery. I took a picture of her sitting in her big chair in the room just before she was taken away. The next time I would see her was going to be much later in the day. She was just there peacefully waiting for the next step. No tears, no sighing, absolutely no sense of fear. I asked her how she was doing and she said she was ready. If you ever wonder whether God is with us in moments of deep struggle, I can say without any hesitation, He was there that morning. The room was "full."

The nurse even asked us, "Are you people of faith?"

I spoke first (of course), "Yes. I'm actually a pastor."

"I thought so." Her response brought a smile to both of us.

The nurse informed me that Becky would be leaving soon and she would be taking me to the first waiting room. She also said I would be assigned a nurse who would be taking care of me for the day. *My own nurse?* They have people there to look after you and keep you informed as to how things were going. They had thought of everything.

I knew we needed to say goodbye and I was trying to think of something real pastor-like to say or better yet, something loving-husband-like to say, but I couldn't get any words out. I just looked at her. For the second time on this journey I was out of words.

"It's going to be okay," she said, "I'll see you later."

And off she went with the attendant down the long hallway in that great big bed.

I walked down that hallway to the room with the nurse who told

> "It's going to be okay," she said. "I'll see you later."

me someone would be coming along soon to take me to the next waiting room. I was alone now. I'm sure many of you are wondering why our kids didn't come? This is a major surgery. What kind of crazy family is this? I suppose looking back we might have planned that better, but it just seemed like something Becky and I needed to do together… just the two of us. Believe me, our kids would have been there in a heartbeat if I would have suggested it to them, but we were alright being there together. I was thinking, *What can they really do if they are here? Just wait.*

They were back home like everyone else…waiting.

I'm not going to spend a lot of time defending that decision but, let me make a quick point. Not every decision you make in difficult times will be the perfect one or, in some cases, even the right one, but we do the best we can at the time. This was never a point of contention with them or us because our relationship as a family is "healthy." We all trusted that God was in control. He will take care of us and He will take care of all the details. We could rest in that peace, and peace was there.

Our girls were highly invested in this. This is their mom! No matter where they were at that moment nothing was going to change that fact. I those moments of decisions you need to know the hearts of those involved. We knew theirs and they knew ours. It was that "family" bringing life to Becky and me through the journey. We didn't have to spend hours wondering what those young ladies were thinking, we knew. You can read it their social media post and when you do, you will hear the deep cry of their hearts to God, and their confidence in His care for all of us. They wrote some powerful words during that time.

Liz wrote:

Ok, friends, here we go with pretty big update on my mom, Becky Teel.
The surgery looks like a go and has been scheduled for tomorrow (Friday) morning, but there is still one stipulation.

In the first hour of the procedure, they will be checking the liver for any signs of cancer. Keep in mind that the scans have all been clear thus far. But they will look at the liver arthroscopically (sp?) to make absolutely sure there is no cancer on the liver. If the cancer has spread, they will close the incision and not finish the surgery. But if everything is clear, they will proceed with that big Whipple procedure.

Mom will spend 9 days in the hospital after surgery, if everything goes as planned. The people at Mayo have been wonderful and have instilled great confidence in my parents. God continues to show His mighty hand in this situation. He is guiding and leading every little thing.

So for now, we ask for prayers for tomorrow morning, specifically that the liver would be clear, and that the procedure would go off without a hitch. And pray for that wonderful surgeon who will be performing this procedure. Praise the Lord for his expertise! Mom is in good human hands...and divine hands. :)

Love and blessings to you all, and thanks again for all of your prayers. I'll try to keep you posted as I know more.

Abbie wrote:

Becky Teel is having surgery tomorrow. In the first hour they will check for any other spots that may have been missed by the scan. If they find any extra spots, they will not do the complete surgery. So, we are praying that there is no spreading and the only spot is really on the pancreas. If so, they will do the whipple. Essentially Dad says he doesn't want to see the surgeon for at least 6 hours after Mom goes in. 😊

So, pray, pray, pray! This is a really big deal. God is obviously moving thus far. Mom's surgeon is actually an instructor for people learning how to do this surgery, so God put her in very capable hands. 😌

We have witnessed God's power and grace and may we now give Him the glory for the incredible work he is doing through the doctors and through our lives. He is on the throne! May God be real for you today, and I mean, really real. Pray up my mama people!!!!

I sat in this new waiting room for only a couple of minutes when I was then met by a nurse who told me she was going to be my attendant for the day. She informed me that her job was to make sure I was doing ok, and if I had any questions or concerns, or even if I wasn't feeling well, I should not hesitate to tell her. She was very aware of what surgery Becky was going through and said she would inform me how things were going.

What we had learned that morning was that the surgeon goes in first with a scope to "take a look at things." Very small incisions are made for the scope to be inserted so the doctor can access the area. Although all of Becky's scans looked favorable for the surgery, the real test was actually seeing the area with his eyes. If the cancer had spread or found its way onto the main arteries in that region of the body, then the surgery was far too dangerous and the entire procedure must be terminated. So even after coming this far and going through all this "preparation," there was still a chance they wouldn't be able to do it. I have already shared what that means in terms of survival; the person will lose their battle to this aggressive disease. That was a fact that loomed large in the back of our minds.

The nurse knew the drill and assured me as soon as she knew they were going forward, she would let me know. I sat down in one of the chairs next to the windows. I had come to discover that waiting room chairs were not the most comfortable. I had my laptop, but who can concentrate on work at a time like this? Not me! So, I just sat and watched the other people in the room. Some were on the phone, some texting, some on computers, and some just sitting there with other family members. Once again, I was in a room with people who were on some new path that day. Together as it were…all waiting.

Becky and I had informed as many people as we could about the pressing need for this surgery to be completed, so I knew people were praying for everything to be "right." I sat there looking at the clock as the minutes moved by slowly. The nurse stopped a couple of times during that first half hour and assured me things were progressing right on time. I was sitting on the far side of the room from her desk so her phone was straight in front of me. At the 45-minute mark she picked up the phone. After a brief conversation she looked at me and gave a big thumbs up.

Whew! They are going in. Becky is going to get the surgery done!

God had heard the prayers of all our friends back home and around the world as well. We had a team of people who had spent time that summer in Ukraine, and the Ukranian church in Boyarka was praying for Becky. It was an impressive prayer team that had been assembled. It had been a long journey thus far, but God had revealed Himself to us. That day at Mayo our prayers were being answered. I had peace about everything. We caught it early! Dr. F is our surgeon! It was all coming together like this amazing God plan. Oh what a story we were going to tell!

I called the girls and told them the news and told them to let everyone know what was going on. Such great news!

I knew it was going to be long day and I was perfectly aware of that. The Whipple takes a minimum of six hours, and I was prepared for an eight hour wait. Later that morning my nurse informed me a room had already been assigned to Becky. She told me I could go down to that wing and wait there if I wanted to. She gave me a quick set of directions to get through all the hallways, and I set off on my adventure weaving my way through the maze of hallways once again. I found my way to the second floor and found this new home which would be ours for the next several days. At this point I had very little idea of what to expect. I believe that was a blessing because what was ahead was going to be a rough road for that poor girl. The surgery is one thing, but recovery is another. It would be a long stay. One that will would try our patience to the max.

Our new home was a two-bed suite. There was another family there and I walked right in and greeted them. I am a pastor. I'm good at this sort of thing. They were an older couple. The wife was sitting in the chair in one of those stylish hospital robes, so I knew right away she was the patient.

I asked her how she was doing. She said she was doing remarkably well for all she had been through. She was hoping to maybe get to go home that very evening. I said I was waiting for my wife to come down and told them she was having the Whipple.

"That's the same surgery I had," she told me.

"So how long have you been in?" I asked.

"This is day five, and I'm feeling pretty good," she responded.

"Great news!" I said.

I told them what I did for a living and we went on to engage in a time of friendly conversation. In a few minutes a couple of doctors came into the room to talk to them. I politely excused myself and left the room. Once again, I was so encouraged by this "chance" meeting with this family. It set my heart at ease and I was much more confident. We can do this! These people did it! We can too!

There was this small room at the end of the hallway which can be used for family members to talk on phones or just sit and rest in a private place. This little "sanctuary" and its quiet walls would become a restful place for us in the coming days. It is not much of a room, by most standards, but it was a place with a door; when closed it removed the sound of IV alarms and the continual busyness of a post-surgical wing. This little room would be a gift to us.

I sat down on the little couch in the room and waited… and waited…and waited. The sun began to come around to my side of the building. The room had two big windows on the west wall looking out toward the street that passed by the west side of hospital. It was actually a very nice view. It was a bright sunny day, and the sunshine warmed the room as I sat there. It made the waiting so much more relaxing for me. The room was positioned in such a way that if I turned away from the large windows, I could look right down the long, and I mean *long,* hallway to a far distant wall. I sat there looking down that hallway waiting for Becky as the hours passed.

Then…

My phone rang. It was my good friend, Marshall. I don't have many close friends. That is my way I guess. I have dozens of people who are friends and many people I absolutely love spending time with, but I have only a small group I consider dear friends. Marshall is one of them. As a pastor, I have to be wise about sharing deep things with others, but often it is more than my professional caution that keeps me from sharing. It is my way of being private. I am not a person who seeks attention. I like my private time and my alone time. I am good with just my guitar and a quiet place to sit and think. Sitting there alone wasn't a problem for me. There are just some people I don't mind talking with because they take no energy. They completely understand who you are and how much space you need. Marshall is that friend.

Here is my point in all of this "Marshall" talk. When you are going through hard times, you need those safe voices in your life, people who don't have to share deep insights or offer some new revelation of deep theological significance. They may not even pray for you out loud, but they are like attending angels. I don't know what the connection is. Maybe it is our personalities that work together or some deeper level of relational kindred spirits. I don't want to over analyze this, but whatever it is, it works. It is nice to tell them and I have!

Those friends were life-giving to me. If you have ever been through this kind of thing you know how important these people can be. I hope I can be that for others because of the difference friends like that can make when the chips are down and life gets tough. Becky had those kinds of friends as well. She too had friends that gave her so much joy and encouragement. I believe that only comes from a friendship that is grounded in something spiritually life-giving.

It had been a long day already so talking on the phone was a nice break from all the waiting. I don't remember any of the conversation partly because I'm sure the content of our words wasn't nearly as significant as the pleasant time we shared. Words can get in the way sometimes. As I sat there looking down that long hallway visiting on the phone, a bed at the far distant end of that hallway came around the corner. (I'm not kidding, this is how it happened.) I saw the attendant pushing this bed down that hallway. It was coming toward me but too far away for me to know who it was. I told Marshall that I could see a bed coming down the "road" and maybe it was Becky. The bed kept coming, passing the nurse's station now and on our side of the hallway.

"Marshall, I think it might be her," I told him.

Marshall said he needed to let me go and we ended our conversation. I was standing now. I could see her. It was Becky! There was something about all that waiting that had touched a deep place in my heart that day. Without even being aware of what was going on something was connecting us in a brand-new way. I'm not trying get all sentimental here, but those were deep moments we were sharing together in our lives. Journeys that are filled with life and death struggles have a way of washing our souls with a kind of holy water that removes all the insignificance of the day. They fill us with a sense of love for the other person that changes everything about the present moment.

I walked out the door and stood over her. She was awake, but very groggy. With a rather slow tongue from all the meds in her system she said, "I was there all day!"

Standing there beside the bed and next to the attendant whom I hadn't really noticed at all, the only words that came out of this well-trained pastor were, "You sure were!" I was so glad to see her.

Here is my post the following day:

A little update for Becky. This has been a fast week of decisions and direction for us all. Yesterday she had the surgery we have been talking about. Nearly 8 hours in length. Her first words to me were, "I was in there all day"...I guess you were.

The surgery went well. The naughty tumor is gone and they have all good margins. Good news for sure. The pathologies will be completed by Tuesday...kind of a big deal. How much chemo/radiation still to come will be determined by that information. It's still a long road ahead, but now we are fighting back.

I thank all of you for your words, the prayers, the support, and just your being there for her in this. It has completely overwhelmed us both. She is so a peace at with this...almost takes your breath away. She will be here for most of the week. Very often there are complications with this procedure..we expect those and this place is so ready to fix whatever comes up...they are so prepared. Her recovery is in the 3 to 6 month range from the surgery...that's right...months. Then of course there is the cancer which has to be battled too.

In my line of work you try to tell people there is something/someone else bigger than anything the world can throw at them...I don't know how many folks buy that idea. I've grown up a lot in the last few years...learned about myself...others...and how to "tap into" this amazing God we have. I'm now trying to teach others about that.

This has opened my eyes to whole other level of what that means and just how extraordinary that can be...
and God is still amazing me.

Becky said..."Go tell 'em Clyde...I am not fighting this for nothing."

I'll do my best... Thanks everyone.

I look back now and realize how many different pieces there were to this surgery puzzle. At the time it seemed as though we had just crossed the biggest barrier of all. The surgery was behind us. All she has to do now is heal up and get on to the next thing. I was so confident that things would be all right. I mean, the lady in the next bed was only in the hospital for five days. We can do this recovery thing at least that well, and if it takes a little longer, we can do that too. Recovery was going to be no simple task, as I was about to learn. There was so much more left to learn in these long days still ahead.

Chapter IV
The Days at Mayo

Recovery

Becky's recovery had started. You measure your success with small steps, which included a number of important first time accomplishments. Each step has its own set of challenges and as we are going to find out with the Whipple, the first major step was going to be getting all those systems in her tummy to start working again. All of the digestive functions had been dramatically affected by the surgery and those systems' responses to this new environment were not going to go very well. Her bed was a typical hospital bed with all the wires, cables, and tubes, and they were all hooked up to little machines with brains. All these little machines were working away each one doing what it is designed to do and each with its own little alarm tone. Oh, the alarm tones! Those things would become very annoying.

It was amazing to me how captivated you become with watching all the numbers and all the functions of those machines. I would watch them so intently as if somehow I could figure any of it out or had any idea what they were doing. To be fair to myself, I did gain a bit of knowledge as to how they worked and what each of them did, but that knowledge was limited. I found a sense of comfort when everything was working properly. I knew somehow it was all a part of getting this part of the journey behind us. We didn't want any setbacks and as long as there were no alarms going off, life was good!

She wanted to talk so we talked a little right away. The pain meds were doing their thing so talking was somewhat limited, but there were things she wanted to share. Our conversations would become all about the different systems. Blood pressures were taken. Blood sugars were checked because now much of her pancreas had been removed so she was diabetic. Pain meds had to be administered at the right time and on and on the list goes. Every little detail had its own set of complications and yet each one was so vital to the overall healing of this girl. I was now becoming a caregiver.

I'm not sure when a person realizes this "caregiver" part has happened, but somewhere in the middle of the journey it happened. I have talked with many other friends on these rough pathways and they all say there was a point when something changed. You discover you are now taking on a new role. It is not as though you are wishing for this *not* to happen or that you are consciously trying to avoid it. It just happens. It never bothered me or made me angry as I know for others that does happen. For me I just noticed that the landscape had changed. I was there for Becky now and I was completely alright with that idea. As a matter of fact, I found it was what I really wanted to do. Motivation was not a problem at all. Every little task was something I couldn't wait to do.

They have those little sponges with water on them and before people can drink they can have a little fluid on those sponges. That was something I could do. I can handle that sponge. How hard can that be? I had to be careful because her tummy was all messed up and we didn't want to give her too much water. Even the sponge had to be carefully monitored. *Be careful now.* Your mind becomes focused on every little task no matter how small because you don't want to mess anything up. This is how Becky is going to get better and get back home again.

I keep going back to this, but it is certainly part of my reasoning for writing this story. I am a pastor. I go into rooms for people in post-surgery all the time. I have visited with people after procedures and I have prayed with them for healing and strength to get through all the tough days ahead. I can do that. It is important for me to be there for them, but this situation is not the same at all. I am a pastor by trade/calling but, I am not a pastor here, at least not like the one who does the preacher stuff. I'm a *caregiver* now. This is Becky! I am not even sure caregiver is the right term. I have said over and over that words and titles fall far short of what we are really feeling. I was doing all of the task not because it was my duty, but because I absolutely could do no less. I was feeling no sense of special virtue like, "Look at me, am I not hitting this it out of the park?" Or "Did I not tell you I'm good at this?" Those thoughts aren't even on the radar. You just go at it! I could think of nothing else I wanted to do at that moment.

The seconds go by. I say that because that is how it feels. You are confident that each day things are going to get better so what you want is time to move quickly. It doesn't. How can days seem to fly by when life is normal and then when you need it to move it stops? The attending nurse would tell you something like, "The next med comes at 10am." Immediately your mind goes into watch-mode for 10am to arrive. You are focused on 10am and once that is finished you are on to the next thing and then to the next thing.

You become so connected to everything going on. Once again, it is not like you are making a conscious decision to do this, it just happens without any effort on your part. This process of caregiving, once started, will continue to be who you now are. Little by little it takes a place in your daily life. It is like a new family member who has moved into the house, and it will reside there until the journey is over.

The first night was a long one. There were all these first things to get done. Becky had to stand at some point. Do I even need to tell you what that was like? She had an 18inch incision that stretched from one side of her body to the other. I can't imagine the sensation of getting up that first time. She did it, but it really hurt. It was our first profound introduction to the word "pain." This is only the beginning. Like so many other issues with cancer, pain is going to become our worst enemy in more ways than we can ever imagine at this point in the story.

I didn't like anything about the pain. I mean, who does? I would become so helpless in those moments. I just wanted it to go away. Now if it were brief moments of discomfort like the pain of trying to get up or move I could handle that because I knew she was doing something to cause it and as soon as she stops doing that the pain will end. But when it was just pain that comes with all the surgery and everything going on inside and when there is nothing you can do to stop it, those are the times that my heart would hurt. With the Whipple there would be lots of those moments. The hospital was well equipped for this of course and our team of nurses, who work with many of these every week, knew what was coming. They did an amazing job of staying on top of things but, no matter how on top of things they were, there would be times when the pain would get a little out of hand.

There was one particular time that stands out in my mind. It was late one evening and Becky's recovery was at the point where they needed to start taking her off the pain meds. Pain meds slow down all the systems in your body and they needed to get those systems working again. It's a delicate balance of dealing with the pain and getting her tummy back to normal again. Sometimes that process goes well and sometimes it doesn't. On this night the stomach cramping wasn't going well and she was getting very uncomfortable. The nurse was doing her best to accomplish what needed to be done and doing a great job of encouraging

Becky to hang in there, but it started getting a little out of hand.

I'm sure some of Becky's trouble was the fatigue and frustration of hours and hours of dealing with everything. It was getting the best of her and she just wanted out of that pain world right now! It was hard to be there. I felt so helpless! The nurse decided to use the IV in Becky's hand to administer a quick acting pain med. I don't know for sure but in her haste to get things under control she might have injected the med a little too fast and...more pain. Becky cried for the first time, "Clyde, pray for me!" It was this desperate cry for help. I had never heard her ever say that and certainly had never experienced that kind of intense need from her ever before. I was paralyzed.

My mind was numb. *Well pray, you fool!* After all, this is what you do! You are a trained professional who can pray in the most trying of circumstances. I had done it before with others a number of times, but this was different. My sense of calm had been shaken by the struggle of someone who wasn't just another person in need. This was Becky.

I told her I was. I thought I was praying, but sometimes there is just not enough room in our minds to capture the moment with the right set of actual prayer words. I was caught up in the emotion and battle of the moment and couldn't find words to offer. I am typically a calm person in tense moments like this. This time I couldn't make it happen.

I have come to realize as I look back that when we are facing these painful times in our lives God is not looking for our *perfect prayer posturing* rather, He is looking for our hearts to come thirsting for water that only He can share. Praying for someone is one thing, but our hearts pleading/ crying for someone is a whole different thing. In that moment I could not manufacture the right words. It then became a combination of being there with someone you sincerely care about and being connected to a God in a relationship that was not clouded anymore by shallow religious overtones. I was praying the best I could! My tongue was stuck, but my heart had never been more connected. *"Come on God, get in here!"*

Becky was a Pentecostal girl. She was not the "praying in tongues in public" type. It was something she told the family she did in private. She said it was her way of praying when she could not think of any words to say. I don't want to get into a speaking in tongues discussion right now. My reason for sharing this is that on that night, in her room during this very rough point, I heard her. She was out of words just like me, but she had that other gear. It was the only time I ever remember her praying in tongues in public. The poor nurse was a little taken back by the whole thing, but I knew exactly what she was doing. In that moment, if you are Becky, you are reaching for anything you can find. The only well she could draw water from was there and she cast her empty heart into that well. God was there!

Then, as if by magic, it would often come. A calm would fill the air. In that crazy mess of a world peace began to settle on us. It happened so many times. I can't explain it all, but I have seen it so many times in the world of struggle. God was there and I knew it. Everything was going to be okay. I loved those times! I hated the broken moment, but I loved being in that "place." It was a long night, but the sun would come up and a new day would be upon us. Another day of walking down to the nurses station as often as she was able. Another day of tummy cramps. Another day of trying to get all those crazy systems going again.

Becky and I got to know the second floor pretty well. For me, traveling back and forth each day from my hotel room and getting in and out of the hospital became an everyday thing. Before long you start to get into a routine. We discovered, as I had mentioned earlier, that little sanctuary room at the end of the hallway. It was literally right next to her room. We loved going in there pulling along the IV rack, and going in to sit down there for a few minutes at a time. It was a quiet place away from all the clutter of the hospital. We spent a considerable amount of time there and talked about all kinds of things. It seemed like going in there made the time go faster, and for some reason, it felt like she actually did better in there. Maybe it was the sunshine in the afternoon or maybe it was simply the room that didn't feel so much like the hospital. I don't know. All I do know is that it provided a place for our lives to rest from all that stuff going on. I know reading through this story you might be wondering why I would even mention this room, and I'm not exactly sure if there is a serious point to it. It was our place at the end of the hall and we never forgot it. It meant something to us, and maybe that's the point. It meant something to us and that's enough.

Let me remind you there is a world going on outside the walls of the hospital. Everything outside those walls was still moving along as if nothing had happened. Life goes on for everyone else and there was a church back in Sioux Falls.

They had all been wondering how things were going. They were praying with such passion and conviction and their concern for our wellbeing would be voiced over and over again. If you will remember we were into this fundraising campaign for our new education wing, and the church leaders decided (with Becky's encouragement) to move forward.

"This is no time to stop!" she would tell me. "I'm not going through this for nothing!"

I know this was not easy for our church family either. They were wrestling through their own questions about all this. Becky and I had been with them for a number of years and we as a couple had stood with many of them through many other difficult times. We were not just *professionally* connected to them. This was a family to us. The girls and I would do our best to communicate back to them what was going on. This might be a good time to let you all read some of the things we were writing while Becky was in Mayo. You will read in those words that we were not discouraged one bit. There were so many people in Sioux Falls who were absolutely confident that this horrible disease would not take Becky's life. Surely this wouldn't be God's purpose for this. Our determination was not wavering. As a matter of fact, I think we were gaining faith speed. The church was growing and the depth of what was being shared was life-changing for everyone involved. In the end, we believed, this would turn out to be a blessing. God was going to be glorified. Can I get an Amen!?

Let me give you a quick update on this Sunday night. Two days behind now on the Surgery. She is pretty tired...no surprise...gaining though. She is an amazing girl with all this. So much yet to do, but she is determined.

I was home for the day just to do church and let me say...we have an amazing church family. It was powerful to be with them today. This is when church is real, and I love it that way.

We will find out more information as the week progresses.

I'll try to keep you informed. Right now, she needs to heal. We don't want any leaks in those places where talented hands were working. Go God Go.

We have all been changed. I think a little everyday. I am in the business now of teaching people what God can do, who He really is, and how to discover the most extraordinary presence in these moments. I wish that gift for everyone.

Thanks everyone for your prayers...it means so much. Miss Becky is not alone...you are all making a difference.

A little update here on Miss Becky. Today was a good day...we've had some tough moments though. We just can't get digestive "things" to get going. This is something that happens with this surgery...but it is not fun. She was a very sick girl for a couple of days and got so worn down, but today was better. She was sleeping most of the day and really resting. Her pain was very much under control and the discomfort of a very upset tummy was being taken care of as well...she was resting.

So now we have to get a good night's rest and then get things working. Once that happens she'll be going home soon, but you never know when that is going to happen...hours...and sometimes even days. It's not something you can really control. Imagine that...like this has been anything we can control at any level.
It has been a long month for us. She said today that the month of September has just passed her by. So much to do...and happening so fast. Once we get home then she'll have days to recover and then we move to step two. Chemo...maybe radiation...the cancer is still there. The battle is on...and on.

You learn more each day here. You learn about struggles and pain. You learn how good a good day actually is. You learn how minutes can become hours. You learn how to celebrate such small things. You learn appreciation of *things at a whole new level. You learn how very silly some things that we think are so important...really are not. I'm still learning.*

Thanks for all the prayers, the cards, the flowers, the phone calls, the concern is overwhelming...thanks so much. We cling to hope the next day may bring, believing and expecting God will show up...He always does...in very amazing moments of peace.

The Concert

While Becky was at Mayo our team back home was working very hard to put all the pieces together for this up-coming concert. We had actually contacted the band explaining to them what was going in our lives with Becky's cancer. We had already received some wonderful messages back from them wishing us all well and letting us know they would be praying for Miss Becky. We knew now she wasn't going to be able to play or to even be there and that was sad for us. Again, a concert might seem trivial in the face of cancer, but this was about more than a concert. It was about who we were as a family. Let me remind you that when you are going through these messy times in your life you find yourself reaching for anything that seems normal again. Ricky Skaggs was coming and Becky wasn't going to get to be there. She wouldn't be playing with us. She was so disappointed.

I suppose there will be some who are going to question our decision to leave her in the hospital and do a crazy bluegrass concert. I'm also sure if you have been reading through the pages of this story you might have a sense now of just why we did. **Becky said go!**

Her sisters came over to stay with her that weekend. She wasn't alone, but if you think it was easy to walk out of that room and drive home that four hours, then you don't know me and you surely have not yet come to understand who Becky was. We talked about this a number of times afterwards and she visited with others about that decision as well.

Becky's answer would never waver, not once. Her determination in those matters had to do with her defeating this ugly disease. Her thoughts and reasoning had to do with never letting this cancer take her life and that meant the one she was living *right now*.

Cancer is an awful disease that robs us of so much in our regular lives. It places so many physical limits on our activities because the cancer disease and even the treatments themselves will steal away what little energy we might have left. It can be so invasive on so many levels, but for Becky it wasn't going to take everything away. In areas she believed she could win, she was going to win. I hope you begin to understand this because that attitude will change your life. God was all over that girl.

I arrived back in Sioux Falls and found everyone working overtime to get things ready. The church was deeply connected with Becky's situation and we were going to do this as well as we could for Becky. I didn't have any trouble getting help. The church people were ready to do anything to make that work. It is still amazing to me how strife can bring out the best in people. The concert was going to be exciting! It was sold out and very up-lifting. Ricky Skaggs was very aware of what was happening and he was on it. I'm sure it wasn't like the typical concert that that band does every day and it was so special to all of us. Our family played at the beginning with our Becky not there. It was hard for us, but we took all that sorrow and let it go. We poured that into our music that night, but we all wished Becky could have been there.

At the end of the concert Ricky, stood alone on the stage and starting talking about Miss Becky. The room became very quiet. God was there. He said he wanted to do a song for her. I quickly grabbed my phone and walked down the side isle of the worship center and called her. I put my phone on speakerphone and stood there. A short guitar intro and then, Ricky sang,

> *"Somebody's prayin'. I can feel it.*
> *Somebody's prayin' for me."*

He sang the song as only he can with that high haunting voice. Our family knew the song by memory. It was one of our favorites. When he finished he said good night to everyone and walked off the stage. I turned to go back down the aisle. I don't remember seeing anyone as I was talking to her on the phone. She was crying. I mean really crying... sobbing. It had really touched her heart. I walked through the door and into our small chapel on my way to the lobby and came face to face with Ricky. He had left the stage and quickly made his way down the side hallway. His only words to me were, "Is that Miss Becky on the phone?"

"Is that Miss Becky on the phone?"

I only nodded yes because I certainly was in no condition to say anything. He took my phone, "Miss Becky? This is Ricky."

He walked off to be alone with my phone...and Becky on the other end. I didn't follow. He came back a few minutes later, handed me the phone, and said something about how special she was. I took the phone. She told me he had prayed for her and had specifically prayed that her tummy might start working pretty soon. That is what we needed to have happen. We needed to get that tummy going. Things needed to start working again. Amazingly later that night, Becky's system did open up. It was working...finally.

Becky would tell us all that what happened that evening was one of the most special gifts she had ever been given. She said it was the best concert she had ever seen. Once again let me remind you as you read these words that God works in ways we can never design. I still wish to this day she could have been there, but it didn't work that way, and I have to trust that His way was the best way. She was waiting back in Mayo for me. I was going back. It was time to bring her home.

A little weekend update on Becky. She is still there. I came home for the weekend to do what I do here and then going back tomorrow morning. She was ok with that. She is doing better each day. Pain meds now are just acetaminophen...pretty good for what she has been through. Her tummy is starting to work, but it is a slow process and if you try to speed things up that only makes it worse. So you just have to take your time. Everything with the surgery seems to be working just fine which is so good. We are nearly done with this first hurdle in the process. Then it will be on to the second one.

Right now it is just do one thing at a time. Thinking ahead only makes the whole thing seem so big. We have been so supported by so many people at so many levels. We are overwhelmed by that. We really are.

Last night Ricky Skaggs and Kentucky Thunder did a show at our church. It was a special night for so many who came and for us it was a time to let go of what has been so pressing on our thoughts. Our family played a little at the beginning...Becky didn't get to play...she just had to sit her room...we didn't like that so much. Ricky did sing a song for her at the end...I let her listen on the phone. She was was pretty overwhelmed with that...a few tears. He talked to her on the phone after that. I thought that was pretty nice. We are trying celebrate in the middle of this mess whenever and however we can.

We know this is all for such a bigger purpose than we can see right now. She said from the very beginning this was never just about her. We can already see that so clearly. I am just wandering how the bigger picture is going to play out....whose this really for? Whose life gets touched by all this. You learn to have Kingdom eyes...it's better that way.

Thanks again everyone for what you bring to our world. You are special.
God told me to tell you.

Chapter V
Going Home

Getting Things Right

Becky had been at Mayo for nearly two weeks. It is not uncommon to have to stay in the hospital for that length of time after this kind of surgery. The Whipple recovery is at the top end of the recovery timescale. She was still having a very difficult time with food and stomach cramping. Before she could go home everything had to be working properly. She was so weakened physically and emotionally by the whole experience. It looked like we were going to do a third weekend at Mayo. It was a Friday afternoon and it was time for me to go back home to do church on Sunday. Liz, our oldest, decided she would come over and spend that time with her mom. By now the routine of it all had become commonplace for us. I know that might sound crazy, but we had accepted this new role and that meant we would do whatever needed to be done. There was certainly no need to get all worked up over the thing.

It wasn't an unpleasant stay at all. You start to enjoy the people around you. The nurses were always so encouraging and when you are there for as long we had been you get to know those nurses quite well. You get to know the whole place pretty well. We knew where they keep those nice warm heated blankets and where they store those fun snacks. They were very special people and we had come to really enjoy their company. I left and made that long drive back to Sioux Falls again. I arrived back home and settled in for the evening. Liz called, "They are letting Mom go."

"What? You mean right now?" I asked.

Liz explained, "Yes, we are getting things ready and we should be leaving here shortly."

I knew that was going to be interesting because it is a long drive from Rochester to Sioux Falls even if you are feeling well. Becky was very weak and lots of things weren't really ready yet. She was still having issues with the cramping. Those cramps would bring a few seconds of pretty intense pain. It seems like you wait forever to get out of those places and then just like that everything is going full speed. All I could do was wait at home for them to arrive. Liz told us all later it was one of the longest trips she ever made in her life. They would drive a bit and then take a break. Becky would take time to move around a little at some rest stop or gas station and then they would get back on the road. Liz said she prayed the whole time. All she wanted was just to get home. I can't imagine what that was like. They arrived back home later that evening. Becky was finally home, but there was so much more to come.

As I have been writing all this down, I have tried to *not* go through every single detail of this journey. I want to share enough to give an idea of the experience and yes, even for you to get a little weary of the battle. I found I had so much to say, but that doesn't mean everyone has that much *listening* energy. I know I have been on the receiving end of that a few times myself. My ears have grown tired a number of times by people who go over and over something until you want to just scream. I don't want any screaming, but I do want to give you all a sense of the size of this struggle, not so you feel sorry for us, but enough so that you begin to realize just how massive and vast some of these things can be. You all have lives that are full too and all of us only have so much emotional gas in the tank. We all have to guard our time because if we bear every burden from everyone who is going through pain we will run out of energy. A good friend of mine has said many times, "There is a million dollar's worth of need in this world and I only have a hundred bucks." The world is full of struggle. We can only do what we can.

Now you might think having Becky home was a time of celebration and it was, but my level of caregiving had to step up a notch or two. I was pretty good when I had those nurses around to help me along. *Just how good am I going to be when they aren't around?* The Mayo folks give you a toll-free number when you are dismissed from the hospital. They encourage you to call back whenever you have a question or concern. I hate making those kinds of calls. I don't want to be calling every single time something happens as if I can't do anything on my own. Who wants to be the wimp that can't figure a few things out on his own?

However, there were times when things were happening and I really didn't know what to do or what was going on. My pride didn't matter. I would call. They were very prompt at returning my calls if I couldn't get through right away. They they were busy people. We were talking back and forth about all kinds of things. One of the big issues was the blood sugar levels. They had removed a portion of her pancreas because of the tumor location, so her blood sugar levels needed to be monitored closely. There was a part of the pancreas still there and the hope was that as it healed it might start working again, but that silly thing was all over the map. For the most part, we handled the blood sugars pretty well, but the one that gave us the most trouble was her tummy. That stomach did not want to cooperate. And there was that lower intestinal stuff.

Can I just pause here for a moment and talk about all that stuff? Sometimes you have to take a little time and try to appreciate the humor in things. We never lost our sense of humor the entire time. There were dozens of moments of tears, but there were times when the only thing you could do was smile. Yes, even laugh at times. We may be fearfully, and wonderfully made, but that lower intestinal function is something altogether. Becky and I knew each other pretty well and we had talked through lots of personal things. You get to know each other like the back of your hand, but we had never taken five seconds to talk about *that*.

However, when you get sick…I mean real sick…cancer sick…Whipple surgery sick, let me tell you, you are going to talk about *that* more than you could ever imagine. All of the sudden it becomes the hot topic of the day from color, to texture, to frequency. My goodness, I am embarrassed to even write it down, but it is part of all of this. Poor Becky, her privacy had just been taken away and all those private things were on display for the world to see. You have to become okay with all of that. You do! As the caregiver you have to step up and do what you can. I am still amazed at what I had to do. And I did it!

For those of you reading through these words who have fought these battles together as a couple, you know exactly what I am talking about. There is a common experience here. Those of us who have been there are like family. I'm simply trying to let the rest of the world in on our little secret. I hope they can begin to see what it is like. They can do it too. We are nothing special. We just did what the situation called for us to do, but don't forget to smile. You can! You must!

Right on the heels of the laughter comes fear. Emotions can turn in a matter of seconds. Becky had been home for only a few hours and things started going downhill. I was checking her temperature and asking her all the best doctor questions I could think of. I had called the Mayo folks on the hotline as well because things didn't seem right. She was starting to run a little fever and the absolute last thing we needed was an infection in her already weakened body. Her tummy wasn't feeling good with that cramping going on, and she was just not doing very well. Once again, I am not trained in this sort of thing so it was hard to know exactly what was happening. But I knew enough to know that this wasn't good. While I was on the phone with the Mayo people it started getting worse. Her fever was going up and she was getting dizzy. The young man on the phone said, "Call 9-1-1."

I made the call. And just like that... down she went. I grabbed her and set her back up in the chair which was her silent cue I guess to get rid of whatever food she had in her tummy. It was not pleasant at all. She was so pale, and I shouted her name, "Becky!" I had never seen her faint before, or whatever this was. That's what is so scary, because you literally don't know what is going on. I have seen surgeries go wrong before and that can be a really serious thing, even when they are the routine ones (if there is such a thing as routine). The Whipple is certainly not routine. What if something had come loose?

It was amazing how fast the first responders came. They were impressive. If you have never been through a 911 situation before, let me just say, those people were awesome. They came in and went right to work. The one guy told us that he was reading about the Whipple surgery on the way over.

"Man, that's an amazing surgery!" he said.

"We already know that. Thanks," I answered.

They weren't sure what was going on either so they hooked up an IV, checked her heart rate, blood pressure and those kinds of things. They made a quick determination that maybe she was dehydrated, but they couldn't be absolutely sure. Slowly she started coming back around again. Now by this time the ambulance team was on scene as well. Obviously, we were going to take her in, but the EMT's said she seemed to be doing okay and if I wanted to drive her to the ER, they thought that would be okay.

I have not mentioned yet that our daughter Liz was right there with us through all of this. Liz is the oldest. Becky and I had Elizabeth when we were in our early twenties. We often tell people that probably Liz raised us as much as we raised her. Liz is an on task young lady. She is a let's-get-it-done kind of girl. So as Becky and I were trying to decide whether to take the ambulance to the ER, Liz broke into our conversation with her thoughts.

"Yes, Mom," she said, "You *are* taking the ambulance!" Okay, decision made!

We loaded up Becky and, of course, just like all towns, the neighbors were watching. They aren't nosy. They were all very concerned about us. Sioux Falls is a large town, but it has lots of small town people. We have great neighbors. By this time Becky was feeling much better, but to the ER she went. After a few tests and checking things out, they also determined she had just gotten dehydrated. It had been a frightening experience. This was all new territory for us and there was no way to prepare for such a thing. We brought Becky home thinking things might get back to some kind of normal, but normal had been redefined and it would continue to change for us.

Dehydration…another word in all of this Whipple business. Becky's upper digestive system had been so messed up that her body wasn't absorbing nutrition like it did before the surgery. All of these important systems had been drastically effected and it simply took time for them to function well again. Eventually, everything starts working, but how that goes and how soon is different for everyone. Becky's system wasn't at optimum capacity yet, and we would have to monitor that very closely. In the next few days this fluid problem was going to be an issue. You could see it coming. She would be a little more tired and then even her speech would slow down. Once I saw those signs I would take her to the clinic. They would hook up an IV and within minutes you could see the change. All you had to do was give her a bag of fluid and she was ready to go again. It was just like filling the gas tank on your car. It was crazy how that would work.

Becky's only job now (which was not a small one) was to heal up and get stronger so we could move on to the next phase of this cancer battle, Chemotherapy. She had some options with this. You can do a combination chemo and radiation treatment or a long-range chemo treatment. She chose the second option. Our doctors told us that their studies were inconclusive as to whether or not the radiation with chemo was any better, so we opted for the chemo alone.

When you look back on all of those decisions you have to make, you realize just how lost you were in the maze of the whole thing. You almost forget the seriousness of the moment because what is before you is this *decision*. You have all these options in front of you, so you reach up and take one off the shelf as if it's some new product line in the cancer supermarket. These are life and death decisions you are making with serious consequences connected to them. You simply have to do your best in the situation. At that moment in time there is just no way to fully understand how it all may go. The doctors involved give you their best information and they do a great job of giving you all the facts and letting you decide. But even after all that, the decision is going to be yours. You are going to decide what is next. Whew!

Jesus, be near because this is hard.

I can remember, after Becky's diagnosis that we were being completely overwhelmed with all the schedules and things to get done. It started to weigh us both down. There were times during the first month when I would just lose control of my heart for a few moments. I would sometimes cry, but I would do it in the shower because I didn't want her to hear. I was afraid she would feel bad for putting us all through this. You can keep it together most of the time, but you can't keep it inside forever.

I can remember a moment early on when she decided she needed to be done working for a while. Becky had worked as a hair stylist at a retirement home in Sioux Falls called Trail Ridge. She had been there for over 16 years so she had become a special fixture in that place. Those people loved their Becky. She did a lot more than hair. She was their friend who helped care for them in that new home. She knew she would have to take some time off, so she made the decision to get a friend to take her place until all this cancer stuff was over. I believe her last day was on a Friday because that was her busy day. She would leave early on those Fridays. I would usually be back in the bedroom getting ready for my day when she would leave. On this last day something about the situation made me stop my morning ritual for a moment and listen.

Becky had this large suitcase that she took with her every day to work. It was full of fresh towels and other business items. It was one of those bags with wheels on the bottom so you could pull it along. As Becky would leave each morning for Trail Ridge she would go down our half flight of stairs pulling that large case behind her. Each step would have a marked *thud* as the case would bounce along behind her. That morning the sound of those wheels hitting each step really hit me. I wondered if I would ever hear that sound again. I know how small that may seem, but that sound was such a reminder of the life we had shared. The sad truth was I would *not* ever hear that sound again...ever. I've thought about that many times since that day.

Spiritually over the course of this first month I would say it was an amazing ride. I was doing my best to keep the church well informed about what was going on simply because I am a caregiver and I didn't want them to get lost in all of this. They needed to be in the loop. With everything going on in the life of the church at this time, I had a significant responsibility to them as well.

Our church family did such an amazing job of caring for us during this awful time. I was wise enough to know the potential of being overwhelmed by a thousand questions and hundreds of offers to help, but these people were amazing. They kept their distance and yet at the same time stayed connected to our battle. It was one of the reasons we decided to let them all into our lives during this adventure. We felt they could be a part of the journey and then better understand how we were doing. It was also an opportunity for me to stay connected to them and let them know I was concerned about their hearts through this too.

Becky was amazing with them as well. The church folks didn't crowd around her that first Sunday to see her (we were worried about that). They all stood back and let her know they cared. It was a powerful moment to see her back in church. It had been a long journey for her. Becky had a place in the church. I mean that literally. We were doing three morning services and she had her spot to sit at all three. She had never missed a Sunday in over 16 years other than a weekend away with her sisters every four years, but that was all. We all got very used to seeing her there. She always sat on my right side in the front row. She was a great team player and a powerful witness to the dedication we felt to this church family and all these friends. It was her spot. She did play in the 9am praise band (remember she's a bass player), and then she would take her seat and listen...three times...same message. Her interest and countenance never changed from 8am 'til noon. I'm not just saying that to make her look good. She loved being there! She was my best critic and my number one fan.

Becky and I had been at Community for 16 years, and in all of those years she had never stood at the front to share a single spoken word to the church. She played the bass in the praise band and sang in the Christmas Choir, but never spoke a single word from the front. That wasn't what Becky did, but that presence of God to my right in that front row was noticed. It was a bigger deal than most of us knew. This will come back later in the story. For now let me say from a pastor's heart that the people we most appreciate in our churches are the ones who bring joy and the quiet ones who follow the vision. They offer themselves without any regard to being noticed and give themselves to that which they feel most comfortable. Becky was not a leader in the way leadership is often defined these days. She was a follower of Jesus. Maybe that's what a leader is, a foot washer. There is a sermon there somewhere.

Chapter VI
Chemotherapy

Post Surgery At Mayo

We had to make a trip back to Mayo for a post-surgery consultation. Becky was not getting stronger. Her recovery was going so slow, which for the most part meant that her energy level was low. It seemed like we were constantly battling fatigue. She knew she had to get going because we needed to get started with this chemotherapy as soon as possible. However, no matter how pressing the need, you simply can't make something happen. There are things you can't control like that. It is not a matter of the will.

I will be the first to say that our attitudes and our wills are powerful tools in healing. I have observed this before not only in healing, but a good positive frame of mind helps everyone around you. These long journeys have enough strength robbing moments by themselves, and the last thing you need is everyone around you being negative and grumpy.

Again, let me remind you as you read, we are positive people. At this point in the story we were very committed to winning the battle. We caught this early. We have a plan. We have had the best surgeon on the planet. Becky has beaten this cancer thing before. We see how God is using this. She is going to win! God was showing Himself in all of this!

We knew our way around the Mayo Clinic so this time things were very different. We were on a new course. Becky needed to get a little more strength so we could move on to the next step. It was the same parking ramp, same elevator, short walk, same piano, and even the same waiting room. We have this thing down! The doctor's checkup went well. They were a little concerned that she was not snapping back from the surgery like they thought, but this is a major surgery. It should get better each week. They also said we needed to get started with chemo right away. We did meet with the oncology team at Mayo, but we asked if we could do the treatments back in Sioux Falls for the obvious reason of distance. The main reason was Dr. M. Becky trusted him greatly. She was comfortable with all the people who worked at Dr. M.'s clinic, and it just seemed like a better fit for everything she was going to be doing. The folks at Mayo were very supportive with our decision and gave us their blessing.

We drove back to Sioux Falls and set up meeting with Dr. M. to begin the next phase of the treatment. Chemotherapy was just around the corner. A new normal was going to be arriving in our lives. I have used that word a number of times throughout Becky's story, but it is so true. Your normal is constantly changing. About the time you think you have found the next place to stand, the ground starts moving again and the plans you set in place all have to be altered.

Today when I hear that someone is starting their chemo treatments, my heart hears those two words in a very different way. I know there are all kinds of chemo treatments out there with some much more intense than others, but each one of them has its own battle ground. I also know everyone responds to these powerful drugs in different ways. You can read and do all the research you want, but at some point you just have to start. *The only way out is through.*

....

Chemo World

Shortly after getting home from the Mayo Clinic, we made an appointment to see Dr. M. He had been in contact with the Mayo doctors the whole time we had been going there so he was completely up to speed with everything that had been going on with surgery. His plans for treatment were right in step with everything the Mayo doctors had suggested. There was no bump in the road at this point. Our appointment with him was very professional. He explained that the drug they would be using was Gemzar. Gemzar is an effective treatment for pancreatic cancer and although it does have side effects, they would do the best they could to help us through them. Of course, there is always a certain amount of risk with any of these drugs, but it was the best choice of the majority of doctors in the country in treating pancreatic cancer. He suggested we put in a port so Becky would not have to be stuck with a needle every time she would come in for a treatment. The therapy plan was to do one treatment per week for three weeks and then a week off. There would be scans throughout the process to see how things were progressing, but our main focus was her cancer marker.

Becky's cancer marker was affectionately (tongue in cheek) known to us as CA #19. I don't fully know what goes into this classification, but it is a universal medical language used to track these cancer cells. A blood draw was taken each month and then analyzed. From that blood analysis you can get a fix on the marker number. The goal of treatment is to get that number to near zero. Becky's marker number before surgery was over 8000 and had now dropped to 155. Good news! The goal over the course of the next six months would be to bring that number down. We had no idea just how fixated we would become on that number. It is amazing how something we initially knew nothing about would become the center focus of nearly every conversation. Our family, friends, and the entire church would be asking, "What's the number this month?"

We made an appointment at the hospital to surgically install her port. With that behind us Becky was ready for chemo. However, I don't know if anyone is really "ready for chemo." It was that same freight train again coming at us ,but the next step was finally here. The Whipple surgery was behind us, and we were moving on.

Social Media on November 15, 2012:

> I'll do a quick update on Becky tonight. She was in surgery this morning early to put in a "port" so they can infuse the chemo medication. That starts on Monday morning. Here we go for chapter two..or three or whatever chapter this is. It almost feels at times like it isn't real and then you are reminded by schedules and those feelings...it has not gone away. So for the next 6 months this will be what we do. There are test that go along with that every 2 months to see how things are moving along and if changes are needed.
>
> Everyone seems to have a different story when it comes to this part. For some people it wasn't too bad and for others it was very difficult. We are learning that is going to be Becky's story to live and her story to tell. No two are ever the same. I guess we'll know sometime next week what this part will be like.
>
> This is one more reminder of just how much of life we can't control. One more reminder to enjoy every day that we feel good. One more reminder of the clear fact that the world we live in is fallen...broken...wounded...and needs

something beyond it to fix broken pieces. We are learning how to be honest with that reality and not run from our fear. Look right at it...and when you think you can't do it...you're right. Then speak from that place to a God who "gets it"...who understands and knows exactly how to bring the most amazing kind of healing to your life. Something deeper than our "worldly treasure" and its shallow illusion of safety...I'm talking presence here. It's really something...if you don't know...you need to go after that a little.

Abbie's post that same day:

Update on Becky Teel: She had her chemo port put in today. She will begin 6 months of chemo treatment on Monday. She'll do one treatment a week for three weeks and then have a week off. We don't know how her body will react. She could be sick for a day or two after each treatment or she could be sick the whole time. We'll deal with that as it comes. So now we pray for strength, feeling good, and platelet counts to stay up so treatments can continue.

We are amazed every day at the ways this cancer continues to bring honor and glory to God. His grace abounds and seems to be spreading.

Thanks to the many of you who continue to pray and offer your help. We are blessed to be "surrounded by such a great cloud of witnesses"! We see God in your caring and feel Him through your prayers. Go, God, Go!

Another Monday

It was a Monday morning. We got ready and drove over to the Dr. M.'s clinic. It wasn't a long drive and I remember that we were talking about the next six months. It seemed like a daunting task ahead. Six months? Why not three? The chemo regimen seemed like an almost impossible task, but I was in "we can do it" mode. One week at a time! I remember saying something like, "I can't wait for the last trip over to the clinic. Won't that be great? We will be done in time for your birthday so I'm going to make plans to go to the Black Hills and stay the week. We can do this!"

We arrived at the clinic and walked in. We didn't have to wait long and we then went back to another one of those little rooms. Dr. M. came in. He explained the regimen once again and asked if we were ready to go back to "Chemo World." (Those were his words.)

The clinic was very well designed. It was a new building with modern looking décor. The atmosphere was more like a comfortable suite than a hospital. There was a long row of recliners that went in a half circle around a central nurses' workstation which was glassed in. There were large windows across the back wall letting in lots of natural light. It was well designed for these tough medicines to be given to people who are in a bad place in their lives. The clinic staff knows all too well how all of this goes and their skill sets are much greater than mere "injectors" of medicine. We loved those girls. They were so good to us.

As we entered into the room we were surprised to find my brother-in-law Scott Jansen sitting in one of the chairs. Scott has been battling cancer in his life for a number of years and every few months he has to get a "shot" of his medication to keep his cancer in check. His treatments work very well. He would come in for a couple of hours, get his meds, and then he would be good for a few months until it was time for the next round. It is a long journey for him as well. We didn't know he was going to be there on Becky's first day, but it was good to see him there. We sat down next to him. It was as if God had planned it all. Becky and Scott could talk shop together. Becky would say later that seeing him there was a real inspiration and gave her a great sense of strength. Becky's chemo regimen consisted of a small bag of steroids first followed by the chemo med. The whole process took a couple of hours. Little did we know this Monday routine was going to be with us for a long, long time. We were doing chemo now.

71

Becky posted to social media:

> *First chemo down.... Got done about 11:00..... Still feeling good, so went out for a sandwich. They said to eat when I feel like it cause that will probably change! Here we go God........*

Each week on Monday we would go in and do the chemo. Then nearly every week Becky and I would go to our favorite Chinese restaurant. It seemed like that was something that tasted good to her on those days. It got to be our regular date day. Mondays were always good days. I think the steroid gave her a shot of energy. It was going to be six months. A person had to settle in for the long haul. Tuesdays would be just "okay" most of the time but usually Becky would start to feel the effects of the chemo. Then would come Wednesday. Wednesdays could get nasty. We found out later in the game that there were more things we could have done to offset some of the issues, but when you are starting this new experience you don't know enough about it to even know what you should ask. Your experience has no past reference so when confronted by some issue your first thought is, "Is this is just how things are?" You just don't know.

Her tummy would hurt, there was a fever with chills, no energy, no appetite…just plain sick. "Chemo sick" we called it. This Wednesday mess would take all her energy for a couple of days and then slowly, as the rest of the week would progress she would start to pull out of this funk. By Sunday she would be ready to go to church. Then Monday came, and we would start all over again. Of course, there was that one free week after three sessions, and what a welcome relief that was. She would plan all kinds of things for that week, sometimes over planned, but I didn't care. I was just glad she could get out and do something.

Becky's particular chemo did not cause her to lose her hair which we were told could happen. Everyone is different that way, but she didn't have to deal with that. When she would go to church on Sundays she looked like Becky. People would say how great she looked and how well everything seemed to be going. In reality, that was not quite the way things were, but we let them enjoy this new joy they were living. It made us feel good to have them feel good, but for Becky there were so many things that she couldn't do anymore.

Our church does a mid-week program on Wednesday night where we invite families to come and share a meal together and then groups break off into class sessions after dinner. It is a big hit in our church! When we first decided to do something like this Becky was the one who thought we should do a meal, a real meal and not just cold sandwiches. She took it upon herself to organize this meal each and every week. It grew and grew until at times we would be doing nearly 300 meals. That takes some planning and a special set of skills. Those are large quantities of food that need to be prepared and this preparing would take lots of work groups to organize. You also have lots of leftovers to look after. We still marvel at how creative that girl was with leftovers. I swear she could make a batch of chili out of any ingredient. The kitchen was Becky's home and doing that meal was her love. Now sadly with this awful drug she couldn't do Wednesdays any more. That really hurt her. It was just one more thing that had to change in this battle.

This changing of your life is one of the most difficult parts of any illness that goes long term. You have to learn to adjust to the disease because the disease is certainly not going to adjust to you. You can gut it out for a while, but you can't maintain that for any long period of time. I would come home on Wednesday afternoon for a bit to see her and get ready to go back to the church. She was usually in bed most of the day. I would go back, lie on the bed next to her and talk about my day and what the lesson was going to be about that night. We talked about some pretty deep things during those "Wednesday Moments." It would get pretty serious in that place, not so much small talk. Then I would get up and leave her there.

I never got over that awful feeling. I would go down the steps and into the garage. Becky would just have to wait for me to come back. She spent a lot of time just waiting like that. I had to keep going because my life didn't stop and she just couldn't do it. There were times when she would just have to try, but it wouldn't work very well. She had brought a blanket and pillow to church and when she got tired she would go into my office to lie down for bit. It was a constant battle. Chemotherapy, though necessary, is no picnic. It is a rough road as anyone who has been through it can tell you. I know there are chemo drugs that are less stressful to your

73

system, but if you have one of those "big ones," it is very hard. People going through it get left out of a lot of things. I do often wonder what that was like being there waiting for me to come home. There were a few times I would have to go home because it got a little too rough. She would usually text me, "Could you come home?"

"Could you come home?"

I wouldn't ask any questions, I would just head home. I would usually find her shivering in the bed. She could get the chills so bad. We did learn how to manage that better as time went by, but it was always there.

She was losing weight too. Becky would often tell people that cancer was a good weight loss program, but she wouldn't recommend it! (Remember…you can't steal our joy!) For all the years I had known her, Becky had to battle her weight. She was one of those unlucky people who metabolize slowly. It would be her nemesis for much of her life. Cancer reversed all of that. Now the most difficult battle was to keep the weight up. You have to eat! I would run to fast food places, that's right, and buy all the bad stuff. What a crazy thing! She had spent so much time and energy in her life trying to lose weight. Now here she was trying to gain, and she couldn't gain! If you ever wonder if the world is broken/fallen just take a look at this disease. It effects everything in a most crazy way. We had to adjust the diet by buying shakes and high-calorie drinks and just pound down the calories. That too became a new normal for us.

I know I have mentioned this several times already, but it is amazing how much of our lives had to be altered for this. Everything revolved around the cancer. Our conversations were about the cancer. This is a life and death battle and you must do whatever it takes. I don't remember once ever getting angry about what it took to win. I know some of you might have had that experience, but I never did. I did what needed to be done. There will be some moments later in the story where other things will begin to take their toll on me, but taking care of Becky was not one of them. I learned how to do a lot of new things.

New roles.

We had defined roles as a couple. We had learned those over the course of 40 years. It wasn't like we sat down and made out our list (although, that probably wouldn't have been such a bad idea). We did life together and I am sure much of how we did life came purely out of necessity. I am also sure we learned a lot of it from the culture having both grown up in typical mid-west homes. Still, it was who we were. I did all the lawn, car, snow removal, remodeling projects, fix things…you know, the "dad" stuff, and Becky did what homemakers do…cook, sew, clean. You all get the picture. I can never remember her ever complaining about that. She was good at being a mom…amazing. I wish I would have told her more often.

I wish I would have told her more often.

Now I was doing her jobs too. I wasn't as good as she was, not even close. But it was my turn and I stepped right up and did it. I didn't say much about it either. My mom told me, "You were raised right." I'm smiling now. I think, *"Mom, you might be right. Thanks."*

Christmas was coming. That is our family's favorite holiday. We absolutely love it. We like everything about it. We love the music, the decorations, and the gifts. We love the whole thing. We don't even gripe at people who don't get what the season is really all about. That's right, we all know there are those who don't get it. We choose to do Christmas the best we can. This first Christmas in chemo world was going to be different, but we were not groveling in despair. We were living each day as a gift and the hope that we celebrated at Christmas was not a wishful kind of hope. It was hope that was certain God was coming to us. There was a sense of joyful expectation.

I thought I would share a couple of update posts in that time…

We put Becky to bed early...she did chemo again today and it's making her pretty tired tonight. 2012...it's been quite the year. It has changed me a little each day. That's been a good thing. God has taken very good care of us...we will wait on Him in 2013 for more of that. Take care everyone. Thanks for what you all have done for us. Have a blessed New Year!

I'll give a little update for Becky.

She is in her second week of chemo now. She is really doing pretty well with all that. It is a daily kind of thing. One seems pretty good and then you have a day when your tummy doesn't feel right and maybe a little extra fatigue. We also know that as you do this over the course of a few weeks that it builds upon itself so we don't know exactly how that will go, but you really do one day at a time with this and see what that day brings. I think I'm learning not to plan too far in advance. Let each day bring whatever each day brings.

We continue to be supported by so many wonderful people and for that we are very thankful. The Christmas season will be a little different this year for us...and some of that will be a good thing. What I mean is...we treat each moment as being a little more special. It's been good for our hearts that way.
It is the next chapter for us and so far it really hasn't been too bad. It is not something I ever wanted her to have to go through, but right now it where we are and we are doing fine.

Enjoy the season everyone. I mean that.
We are.

Chapter VII
Keep Going

2013

It was the beginning of 2013 and a new year. I remember wondering what the year was going to bring to us. I hope you are beginning to see that we had great faith in Becky's recovery. We didn't know what was ahead, but our confidence and her confidence were so high. The struggle had been long and those first few months had been such a blur to us. We had all gone through so much, but it seemed as though God had something greater for us still ahead. I was surrounded by such amazing people. I had seen God using all of this in such a powerful way to change lives and purify our focus as a church family like it had never been before. It had been a difficult time, but the journey seemed to be one more step in some right direction. Still there were questions on our minds, and some of those would be no closer to being answered at the end of 2013 than at the beginning.

We moved on week by week, one day at a time. Some days were not very good and some were okay, but just okay. I said earlier we were tracking a number. The cancer marker number: CA #19. We would go in once a month and do these tests and check the numbers.

At first there was a little improvement. We saw the numbers dropping a little and then it would go up, but only slightly. The discouraging news with that was she was going through all this misery and not making any progress. The whole point of this was to get the number to near zero, but at this rate we were not going to get there. Still, the only option we had was to keep going. It was the only thing we could do.

Our journey through these months was marked by many ups and downs. We stayed very confident even when she had to make a trip to the hospital because a fever had managed to take hold of her. I could call the Mayo clinic whenever I needed help, and when this fever spiked they suggested we take her to the hospital. I thought I would let you read some social media posts at this time to get a picture of what that was like for us.

On January 9th I wrote:

Miss Becky is in the hospital tonight. We are not sure what is really going on. She has a little fever and an elevated white count and really tired. We are testing to see what's going on. It might be the flu. We are not sure and it's best to be proactive on these things.

So

Put in a little prayer this weekend for her. I have a wedding this weekend and a huge day on Sunday. We just smile at how these things go.
We are not defeated... Not even close. Thanks everyone.

January 13:

A quick update for those who might not know. Becky is home now. She feels much better. Just a little tired. We really don't know the root cause of the fever, but we know we caught it early and headed off a potentially more serious condition. Tomorrow is Chemo Day again. So many of you who read this understand all too well the ongoing journey of this cancer path. We are both learning...not the most fun lesson in life, but it's one that will change you. Abbie posted some very nice words about her mom today...that was nice to read.

Today is Liz's Birthday. Her mom was in the hospital and we didn't really get to celebrate too much this weekend. She took that with such grace. We have some amazing kids...lots of you know that. We are blessed. Life is good. We are all learning as we go. Thanks for the prayers and support. It matters so much to us. We are moving forward. I'm discovering "gears" I never knew I had. Gifts they are...and those "gifts" I will use to tell people what is real and just how amazing God is when you really need Him.

She's home.

Tomorrow is another day. We are not alone.

Abbie would write on the same day:

Update on Becky Teel: Dalton and I picked up Mom at the hospital around 12:15. She and the fam went for lunch at the Golden Bowl. All of her flu and blood tests were negative, but she is taking a 10-day antibiotic just to be sure. No news as to why her white blood count went up. She was able to rest well while at the hospital, so her energy level is better too. She will have chemo tomorrow again, so hopefully her body (and mind) is ready for that.

Many, many thanks to the (what I believe to be thousands of) people who are praying for my precious mother. She is an incredible woman of God who allows Him to do His work in, around, and (now definitely) through her. We know this journey is not about Mom, but one can't help but marvel at watching God at work in her. Dad's life in Christ is just as incredible, as he stood in his pastoral role this morning, wife in the hospital, preaching the power of the Holy Spirit and the gifts He gives out of love. I believe it is the power of all of your prayers at work, together with the Spirit, bringing my parents through this incredibly trying time with such Grace.

May God be seen in your world this week as He works in, around, and through you. Blessings!

Things were never simple. Something was always happening. You have to keep your head very clear. There was a month in the process when the numbers went up to over one thousand. Looking back on this the doctor thought maybe the blood draw that month didn't go right. He thought it might have been a lab misread or a false positive… something like that. Of course the high number really set us back emotionally. In the next month we were hoping that would change. The next month the number dropped to 600. It was a celebration day for us. Even though we didn't know what was going on in the big picture of everything at that point, it didn't matter. We had a good report. I would write that day about celebration:

I'll give my friends a little update on Becky. She is now into the last 3 months of her chemotherapy. However, there is more good news for the week.

Last week they did a CT scan to see how things were progressing. It came back all clear. Also...the cancer marker 19 which had been elevated...started dropping this month from nearly 3000 down to 600...very good news. It has put a new smile on Miss Becky's face as you can imagine. It wasn't very much fun going through the surgery and all this chemo stuff and then seeing elevated numbers...that is very discouraging...but now there is a change. It makes such a difference.

We know the road is yet long. Cancer has a mind of its own. We are learning that, but when you have good news and when you are winning...you celebrate. So for all the prayer warriors out there this is a day to celebrate.

Today she is in getting more chemo, but there is a new smile of confidence in those eyes. It's a big deal. It does my heart good to see her that way. She has been through a lot in the last six months.

Thanks God for the days in our lives when we can see the victory. We thank you for the days we all get to celebrate with those who have good news to share and give us the strength to stand beside those who continue to struggle. We are thankful that you are right in the middle of our lives...we can't do it without you.

One by one the days would pass and we could see the end coming. We were into the last series of chemo treatments. We had done it! Those six months had been filled with all kinds of battles, but that was about to come to an end. There was going to be a new day ahead of us. We knew the marker number was still a little too high, but we had come to believe that maybe they would simply have to do maintenance level of treatment, whatever that was. The main point was that something was going to change, and that was what we were looking for. This new normal had been a long road and we were all looking for some relief. The tone of our voices was different as we shared the news. Everyone around us was ready for a change too. The world seemed to be better now. Maybe we were just naive or maybe overly confident, but it sure felt good to write about something other than bad news. April 27, 2013:

I thought on this pretty spring morning I would update our friends on Becky's journey. She has now finished her 6 months of chemo treatment. It has been an amazing road to observe and be a part of. I know I've expressed several times how I will never use the phrase "chemotherapy" the same ever again. It is a necessary, but tough thing to watch people go through.

So the next step is that she will go in on Monday for more testing and then another doctor appointment the following Monday to go over the options for this next part of her journey... if there needs to be anything more. Our concern has been a cancer marker that is slowly going down, but has not yet reached the level the doctors are comfortable with. It needs to be zero. I've shared that with you all before. She's getting there, and we are praying she'll be there this time. That's a big prayer deal.

We do know that whatever happens with that number something will change in the way she proceeds. If that number is still up a little then they will do a little more chemo...but it can't be as often. That will help for sure, but we would love to be done. I'm sure you understand why.

We are pressed at times, but not crushed, perplexed, but not in despair. Do you know that verse? We are not destroyed. We fix our eyes on that which is eternal...those are powerful verses which have so much meaning to us right now. The world cannot win...for we have this treasure in these jars of clay and we will not lose heart.

Thanks everyone for being there for us. We continue to walk with you in our hearts. Enjoy your friends and family. Thanks everyone for your prayers. Go God Go!

We drove over to the clinic for the 6th month check-up. Remember, we weren't thrilled with how the numbers looked, but we had made it this far. I remember going back to the room and waiting with such a sense of relief. We both knew something was going to change. It was what we had been sharing for several days now. Dr. M. came into the room and went through the normal routine of checking the computer.

"Well, the number is still up," he said.

Becky replied, "We are finished, right?"

"No," he said, "we just keep going. The marker isn't down."

We just keep going?

I remember being so disappointed for Becky. A major surgery, six months of chemo, and all the other battles that she had gone through. Even as you read through these pages *you* are probably ready for a change, but that was not going to happen. At least not at this point. But I wondered, *when*?

All of this happens while life goes on. Life doesn't go on stand-by when we go through hard times. Certainly some parts do, but most of our lives have to keep moving. If you will recall at the beginning of this journey the church was working on a major campaign to build a new wing. While we were going through all this mess, the church was growing and doing great! People said that they had never heard me be so focused and so "on message." It was as if God was using all this to bring us closer together. It seemed to us that God was doing even *more* for His Kingdom now than if life had just been normal.

On her birthday Becky wrote these words:

> *I feel so blessed to get to have another birthday. It's been quite year, but God has been so faithful and good to me, as have all of my friends. Thank you...... Thank you.*

And then she forgot us, her family, so she wrote this back:

> *I left out my family on my first post!! How could I do that!*
> *They have been amazing this past year and I couldn't have*
> *done it without them!! Love you all!!*

That all made sense to me. I knew that truth in my heart, but it was a crushing truth. God was using this to bring Glory to the kingdom, I could not deny that for a moment. That is what He does! He takes hard things, tragic things and builds new hearts with them. He was doing this in ways beyond anything we could ever do on our own. The campaign was a huge success and all the pieces of the project were coming together. It was a great time of celebration in the church. I know how crazy that may sound to some, but hundreds of people were watching it happen. You will hear that reflected in the words I wrote after we found out the news that Becky would have to keep going with her treatments.

> *An update for Becky Teel.*
> *Today we went to find out what is next in this cancer*
> *journey we have been on for the last 8 months. Our hopes*
> *were that the cancer marker would be low enough that she*
> *might be done with this stage of the treatment and move*
> *on, but that didn't happen.*
>
> *There is good news though. The number is slowly falling*
> *which is what we need, but it's not at the level they feel*
> *comfortable with at this point. We also thought maybe the*
> *dose and frequency could be changed, but not this time.*
> *The advice was to continue doing what we have been*
> *doing thus far and work on that number. So...we're moving*
> *forward. They will check each month and see where things*
> *are and once we have reached that low mark then she'll be*
> *done.*
>
> *She has great confidence with this doctor. He's the same*
> *person who took her through her breast cancer in 99.*
> *Confidence matters in these things. We both feel like we're*

on the right path, but it was a little disappointing to get to this point and then realize we are not quite there. The choice was really pretty simple. You go on with it, because that's really the best thing.

So...we need to get the number down...we've always known that, but now that's the target. We keep doing this until we're there. So...there is the prayer challenge before us.

Thanks everyone for following this journey and the amazing steps we have all taken in this. There are so many things in life to learn. So many deeper places we need to be. I am often surprised by how at peace one can be in the midst of a storm. I'm not going to say this is easy or try to make it sound like there are never any tears...but I'm just sharing for those who will listen...don't ever let someone tell you there is nothing to learn in the valley...'cause there is...and I am learning what is there may be more powerful than anything we gain on the mountain top. It's been something. We are so full. Thanks to everyone for the blessing you are to us. God is really big!

It was a new day in this journey. The focus wasn't just on a number. The focus was on the fight we were in. I started telling people that what Becky was going through was like having the flu for nine months. I really don't know how she did it. Each month we would go in for a test and each month it seemed the test would come back with a little higher number. What was going on?

Shouldn't we be able to see something on the scans?

They would do a scan and the scan would come back clear. It was all very confusing and troubling, but we were not giving up. Becky still believed all of this had a greater purpose. She and I talked, and we talked a lot! She would always say she knew it was all for something greater, but we were in a battle for her very life. I know we had always been in that fight, but now the landscape was different.

The Cancer seemed to be winning.

A post in July:

It has been a while since I posted anything about how
Becky Teel is doing...our girls keep everyone in the know
pretty well, but I think it's time for me to add a little
something for those of you who have been so faithful in
reading these. We are always so moved by the many faces
who respond and the many words so nicely chosen. We are
very thankful for all of you. It's a big deal to us.

Today we went in for the number check again...we want
those going down...but they were up a little again this
month. That's not the right direction for her to be done with
this chemo thing. So...on we go...more of the same. It is
pretty amazing how you get so "ok" with news like that.
After some time has passed with this and after going
through so much you just go on...'cause that's really all you
can do. You just have to keep going. I certainly do feel
bad...I do for Becky...this has been a long long road for
her...but even she can respond with such calm in this.

We did get to have some time away with the kids this past
month. That was good...and very much enjoyed. She gets
this week off this week so that she can attend her family's
reunion without being so sick...a gift too. Her Dr. was just
fine with that. You learn to enjoy the simplest things at the
deepest levels. I guess that's been one of the "gains".
It's been nearly 10 months since this all started. It really
does become a "new normal" if that makes any sense. It's
what our life holds and so it's what we journey through. Not
angry, not so frustrated...certainly not afraid. Just learning
and sharing what we can to those who are listening. So
many people who have so much going on.

So...we're good...we're doing fine...a little disheartened I
suppose, but not without a sense of great purpose. I'm
always trying to say things that don't sound so "typical
preacher guy"...but when you are in these kinds of things
it's pretty real...and I keep telling you...God is too...He's not
just a good idea or well thought out life view...He's an alive
indwelling unshakable presence that never leaves us alone
in the dark...I have so learned that. I pray that gift for all of
you reading this...you can't imagine how much. Thanks
everyone...you have been so good to us. Blessed

Becky wrote this in July:

> *The steroids I get with my chemo are keeping me awake,*
> *so everyone that comes to mind is getting prayed for at*
> *this early morning hour!! I serve an amazing God!!! I feel*
> *so blessed.*

....

Our 40th Anniversary

Then in August we saw a little change. The numbers went down for the first time in in several months. Could this be the break we were looking for? Our anniversary is August 4th. It would be our 40th. We decided not to plan anything special because we didn't know how Becky would feel.

On the evening of our 40th anniversary I wrote to our friends on social media. I think I wrote more for my own healing than to give people information. We (the girls and I) were writing to express what was happening in our hearts. We were being changed. You can read it in the lines of each post. This journey was changing us and you could see it in what we were writing. Our faith, though tested, was still rock solid. Our 40th anniversary was on a Sunday as I sat down to write.

> *I thought I would write an update for Becky this evening.*
> *Most of you have probably seen the picture of the family*
> *today and have read the post by the girls. Today is our*
> *40th anniversary. I have absolutely no idea where those*
> *years have gone. We were just kids then…I was so*
> *unaware of what being married was all about. I did the*
> *best I could I guess, but that poor girl had to live through*
> *a lot of silly things. I wasn't always the most spectacular*
> *example of a good husband…and after all these years…*
> *we're still friends.*
>
> *This year has been a tough one for her and this cancer*
> *battle. She did have some good news this past week with*
> *that marker number dropping more than any other*

previous month to the lowest level since she started. If you remember it had gone up the three months before...so it was a good "word" for her this time...something to celebrate in the middle of this journey.

I'm writing tonight because tomorrow she starts her 10th month of chemo and this past month was not a fun one. She was really tired and so sick on some of those days. It's hard to watch. I don't care who you are...it will be grow you up. The conversations we have now are so "full." I have come to appreciate so many things at such a new level and I am trying with more passion than ever to tell people to hold on to the best life brings and celebrate the gifts you are given each day.

It is Sunday so of course I had to go to work.

It was a good day. We spent it doing what we both love to do...be there for our church family and for them to share with us. It's a big deal to us! Becky looked fine...no sign that cancer and chemo have battled with her the past few days. It does my heart good to see her feeling better. I can't find enough words to thank all the people who have so deeply touched our lives this past year. I mean it! I can't give enough back to those close friends who give so much. You know who you are! So I pray that each set of eyes reading across these words are introduced to the One who has taught me to say... tonight...it is well...it is well with my soul. Blessing everyone. Go God Go!

However, if you really want to be rocked a bit, here is what Becky wrote on our 40th anniversary:

Today is the day. 40 years! We've done it all.... For better for worse... For richer for poorer.... In sickness and in health... We love and cherish one another... I pray we can wait many years before we do that last part! It's been a great ride!

That very same week the builders started working on the new wing at church. I marvel at the timing of all of this. I know it looks like crazy timing, but you could see God working all around us. It was so evident. God was in the middle of every single day of this journey. We never doubted it then, and we have not doubted it to this very day.

August would pass, and then September would come. It would be the end of the first year of Becky's cancer. We had now dedicated an entire year to this awful disease. There would be another marker number check coming in September. Now if you remember, the last test in August showed a significant drop in the marker number. Well...in September it was back up to 1100.

Are you tired of this yet?

Becky would write:

> *Another afternoon/evening in bed! That's 3 in a row, and this is supposed to be my good week ! Running a bit of a fever too. Guess I'm complaining , no saint here!*

I don't want anyone to read through this story thinking, "Well they just gave up." We didn't give up. I will tell you there were days when we wondered what was going on, but we had this idea that somehow it was all going to work out. We were confident it would turn out in a whole different way.

Social media post on September 3, 2013:

> *I read through what my girls have written about our day. We have raised some pretty amazing young ladies. If you haven't read them...do. Becky's cancer number went up to 1100...not such good news.*
>
> *We are all on a road that was a little rough today. It was just a year ago that Becky got this bad news for the first time. One year...and we're still here. Today was not the kind of news we really wanted to hear. Rising numbers in the midst of the mess she is wading through does not bring much "joy" to the journey. I felt bad for her. CT scan on Thursday to see what's going on in there. We'll know more on Friday.*

So...

Celebrate the gifts you have. Each day. Every person. Every moment. I think I've said a hundred times this year "You better have something bigger in you life than your circumstance"...cause at the end of the day we're all going to come up a little short. We have tried to teach our girls that God is bigger than your life. We have tried to show them He is a personal, life sustaining presence...even when life is a little empty. Oh yes, I can be empty too...days when I can't fix every problem...days when I'm not sure...days when I can't see far enough to know how things will go, but I'm not going to give up. I'm going to ask God for the grace it takes to do this...He has never failed me yet. I have friends, and you know who you are...who have been such wonderful gifts to me. Thanks to you and the hundreds of prayer warriors out there.

Pray for the journey...that we can all learn something new together that will change the world around you. I wait for God to show me the next step. Thanks everyone who reads...you are all very special.

Abbie wrote that same day.

Update on Becky Teel: Mom had a rough week this week, even though it was her week off. When she went to see Dr. M. today, she found out that her number jumped to 1100. Dr. M. wants to do a scan on Thursday, just to be sure her body is still clear of cancer. She'll find out the results of the scan on Friday.

So, how are we doing you ask? Well, we've definitely felt better than we do now. We are a year from diagnosis is all. I know the cancer battle can be long or short. At this point I'm glad we are only a year in, but also that we are a year in. (Hope that makes sense.) With pancreatic cancer, many people don't even get a year into their battle. We are all fine, even though tears do get shed. They're healing in themselves.

> *Let's ask this question instead, since we all know Mom's cancer isn't about her or us...How big is our God? He is definitely big enough for a number. He's even big enough for the scan. We are learning to walk with Him step by step at each juncture. As Mom said today, "You try to not expect anything anymore, but sometimes I'm still surprised by what we find out." It's true. Our only constant in this whole ordeal is the love of God and the grace he continues to bestow on us. We feel His presence as we talk with one another and hear from each of you. Again, we are not defeated and Mom is not defeated. Sometimes it's hard to grasp how long, how wide, how high, and how deep the love of Christ is, even when you are on the receiving end. He overwhelms us with His love and there is no greater comfort, especially than that of knowing that absolutely nothing can separate us from the love of God.*
>
> *Yes, we know Mom's number is up, but God's love surpasses it. I pray that you all will feel the depth of God's love and know this love that surpasses all knowledge. It is life giving and soul freeing!*

Becky's words:

> *Well, my ca-19 number was up again, about 300 points. Some of my blood count numbers were a little too low, so no chemo this week. First time that has happened. Only God knows what's really going on. Putting my trust in Him. Please keep praying......*

December had come and Becky found herself in the hospital due to some swelling of her intestines. The walls had thickened for some reason. No one really knew what was causing this issue. She was in the hospital again. It would be just one more thing with all of this. There were more tests and just like we expected, the tests showed the marker up a little again, but nothing else. The doctors said it might have been something with the meds or maybe even something in her diet. It was just another one of those things that can happen.

We enjoyed the holidays. Life was going on and we were still trying to do what we love to do. We sing! We did another concert with Gordon Mote at our church. Becky even got to play in that one. We had a wonderful time and then the very next day, she was back to the hospital. Her blood counts were low. It was a crazy week.

Christmas Eve came. Our family doesn't sing much during the year at church, but on Christmas Eve we always do a little program with a beautiful communion service and all the music. That service is one of the best gifts we give to our church, and Becky got to play. It was so special.

2013 was coming to an end but this journey was far from over. I wouldn't write any social media updates again until 2014. We just kept going…and going…and going. The girls slowed down their writing too. Becky was getting pretty sick from the build-up of the chemo drug, but each week she would try to rally for church. 2013 would come to an end with no end in sight. We were all wondering what the new year was going to bring.

God, please show us something.

Abbie would write about it this way.

Update on Becky Teel: There's been kind of a lot in the last week, so I'll break it down list style:
Monday: CT results clear, hemoglobin low, C19 marker up 80 more points
Tuesday: Blood transfusion to increase hemoglobin
Wednesday: Admitted to the hospital due to swelling of intestines (no pain)
Thursday: Bacterial tests came back negative, biopsy of intestines taken
Friday: Released from the hospital at 11am, played a concert at noon☺
Saturday: Uneventful, thankfully
Sunday: Sang in both choir concerts at church and the children's program
Today: Had chemo.
We still have no explanation for the intestinal issue and they are still swollen.

> *I don't really even know what to say at this point. I have been pleading with God, "Don't let me miss the glory" in all of this. Seeing Mom in the hospital on Wednesday night, was a chance to experience the Glory of God. She was at peace and even laughing at Dalton's ridiculous jokes. It was a time where the five of us were together in her hospital room and enjoying each other's company, as we so often get to do. We do not take these times for granted, for we know each and every day is a gift. What a precious gift we have been given this Christmas season! Don't miss the Glory!*

Abbie referenced a song that Gordon sang. It is a wonderful gift that music thing. What a wonderful man he is!

Becky wrote on December 30th:

> *As I sit here getting chemo pumped into me, what a great feeling to know that God is in control.*

Chapter VIII
Something Is Changing

2014

Abbie believed she was being led to write a daily blog for 2014. She didn't really know why, but she felt God was leading her to write a daily devotion. She had a way of expressing herself that seemed to be capturing people's hearts, and so she started her journey blog in 2014. She said it was just for 2014 and then she would stop. It would become an amazing journal of things going on in her world. This was going to be one of the most difficult years of her life, and as you read the pages and pages of text you could see her heart. This was her mom. This was her God. I will quote some of it in the next section of Becky's story, but if you get a chance during or after reading this, take time to page through the blog. There are some challenging words from her.

Abbie's Blog Address: http://abbiecoffey.blogspot.com

Our daughter Liz expresses herself by writing as well, but her greatest expression comes through music. She would write some of the most amazing songs during this time. God was tugging on her heart through this and it would come out in the words and melodies of her songs. She would sit down on a Sunday morning in front of the church and teach us a new song. Most of us didn't want to sing along or even play. We just wanted to listen to her sing. Music has a way of expressing what words alone can't fully express.

I was doing church. 2014 would be the most difficult year of my life. I would cry more tears in this year than I ever had in all my life. On January 1st I had no idea what was coming. The rough road was still coming at us, but our faith was strong, challenged for sure, but we knew God was up to something. We could see it happening in church in the lives of people who were being touched by this unfolding story. We were struggling and the people around us were being blessed and moved. It is not easy to define how that works. I only can express what I was seeing.

January would be more of the same routine with those three weeks of chemo and then a week off. Each month we would go back to the clinic to do another blood draw with an occasional CT scan. In January they decided to schedule another scan for early February. You get used to the routine of scans and blood tests and how it all goes. For months now it was the same. The scan will be clear and the numbers will be up. We just keep going.

But this time there was a change. We are now to the month of February. If you have been keeping track of the calendar, this has been nearly 15 months of chemotherapy. Even then, we were not defeated.

The church in 2014 was going strong. I would often say, "If you do what I do, it can't get any better than this!" The spiritual health of the church was life-giving. The new wing was coming together ahead of schedule and now they were starting the finish work. It looked like we would be able to do a few weeks of classes in the children's wing before summer break. It was a great time at Community! I was deeply focused on my preaching and teaching. It was all good in that place, but at the same time Becky's story was unfolding. Those two stories seemed so unrelated, like two different paths, but we could see so clearly there was a connection.

....

Back To Mayo

What was the change in February? The test showed the marker number was up, which by now was no surprise to us, but there was "something" on the scan. It was small, but it was there. This was *my* birthday week.

Really God? Now?

Becky and I decided to make a trip back to the Mayo Clinic. It wasn't as if we had given up on Dr. M., but we thought we should check all the options and that seemed like a reasonable place to start. Dr. M. was completely supportive of our decision, and we set up an appointment to go back to Mayo.

This was a difficult time. Becky had gone through so much and now there was this new thing. My head was spinning because I didn't really know what was coming next. I was taking time to talk about it with people I trusted. You can't do these crazy things alone. That is not wise. I had close friends in my life, as I have mentioned earlier, and at this point in the story I was so thankful for them. It was as if

God knew I needed a special friend or two. I was blessed to have them. There were some things I didn't want to share with my girls because they were doing their own journey. Sometimes I just needed to talk about things, anything really, it didn't matter.

Everyone we knew changed when we said the scan showed something. This was not the news any of us wanted. When any cancer comes back it is not a good thing. Cancer usually comes back with a greater determination the second time, and I also knew with this one it is almost always fatal. It was the first time I started wondering where this was going. I started wondering if we were going to lose her.

Becky still was not worried. She was still convinced this was *not* going to take her life, but I could tell she was thinking about something. It was the first time I saw concern in her eyes. When people struggle with physical pain, that's bad enough, but this was different. This was a new kind of pain and it had a life of its own. The landscape was changing for us again. I didn't like it one bit, but we needed to press on. So back to Mayo because they might have an answer.

We made the drive back to Rochester. We knew exactly where we wanted to stay. It was now in the dead of winter and they had been hit with a major snow storm. There was snow everywhere. We could hardly maneuver to get into our hotel on the outside of town, but we made it, our second little home away from home. We're back.

The next day we were in the clinic for a couple of blood draws and another scan of course. However, our first visit with the doctors took an interesting turn. They decided they wanted to try to get a biopsy of the small spot to determine if it was indeed cancer. We were ushered off to another part of the clinic and began to make preparations for this procedure. It all seemed like a good plan and once again, I was hopeful this new plan would give us some answers. We had been at this for a long time, but any help was going to be appreciated.

They took Becky back to the room to get the biopsy. The nurse had explained the procedure to us. The doctor would use an ultra sound machine to see the spot. Then using an instrument, with the aid of a computer, he would try to hit the mark with the needle. It all sounded so simple. However, she did also warn us that they might not be able to do it if the doctor thinks it is too risky. It is risky because the location of that small tumor lies in an area that is filled with all kinds of arteries and veins. You could hit one of those, and that would be very dangerous.

It didn't take long and the doctor came out to talk to me. "I am not comfortable doing this," he said. "It is just too dangerous, and I'm not going to try it."

It was an outpatient procedure so Becky was ready to leave in only a few minutes. We now would be staying one more night, and visit our oncologist at the Mayo Clinic in the morning. I had so many questions filling my mind.

Questions. It seems like all we ever get is more questions.

It was a quiet night. However, I am sure I was talking because that is what I do. Becky was reading because that is what she does. Tomorrow would come.

We drove back over to the clinic in the morning. It was a cold morning in Rochester that day. We drove over to the parking ramp and found a great parking spot. I didn't brag this time. Over to the elevator, under the street…out into the lobby…into the Mayo clinic…past the main desk…didn't need to stop because we knew where we were going…past the piano…someone playing again…this time it was a Broadway song…down the hallway…up the elevators…8th floor…turn left…another waiting room.

The nurse calls out, "Becky Teel."

We both walked through the doors into a smaller room… waiting. Another nurse comes in to do a couple of vital sign things and asked Becky her name and birthdate. "Becky Teel. Six, eighteen, fifty-three."

In comes Dr. G. She is so fun! (Remember her?) She bounces in and immediately we were both smiling. She pulled up her chair right in front of Becky and started talking. Becky and I hadn't discussed much about what we thought she might say. It seemed rather pointless now anyway. This crazy cancer thing hasn't gone at all like we thought, so why bother trying to figure something out before hand?

She started in, "Becky," Dr. G. said, "you need a break! I looked at all of your tests. First your cancer marker number is 600." (It had been over a year since the number

"Becky, you need a break!"

96

was that low.) "And the small tumor? It is so small that I don't think we need to worry about that."

My mind is racing with questions.

She goes on, "I'm more concerned with your kidney numbers. Let's focus our attention on that. Those numbers are looking serious."

And I thought, *"Kidneys? Are you kidding me? 600? The marker is 600? It hasn't been 600 in months."*

Once again, we are in this crazy ride of emotion. We were getting *good news*, but something isn't adding up. She went on to say that Becky needed to take a couple months off from the chemo. She said we needed to get back to Sioux Falls to see a urologist to begin working on that kidney situation because left unchecked that could a more serious situation than the cancer. I just kept thinking,

"So now it's not cancer we have to be concerned about? It's a kidney thing?"

Becky just sat there too. I think she was too stunned to even know what to say. The doctor said we could should pay close attention to things, be watching for symptoms. When I asked her what those symptoms were she politely said she wouldn't tell me.

Ah...I see...if people know what the symptoms were they start feeling them. It is like wondering if you are getting hives, and suddenly your entire body wants to itch. I get it.

We both thanked her for the information and walked out of the hospital. We made the decision, even though it was getting late in the day, to drive home. It would be late when we got home, but being home was just better. So off we went back to Sioux Falls.

Now, I know what you might be thinking. *Great news!* It appeared like everything was moving in the right direction, but something didn't seem right to me. It is really hard to explain. Becky wasn't settled with the news either. First of all, we had to go back and start working on this kidney issue. Apparently now this was a pretty serious problem.

However, there was something else. There was that spot. Yes it was small, but that small spot was the reason we went back to Mayo. How can things be okay? It's not as though we were questioning the doctors at Mayo. It was this deep feeling of *"what is going on?"* Those numbers were going up and now they were down to one of the lowest points since way last spring. Really?

I don't know if you can fully appreciate this, but even good news has a "be careful" filter when you have been battling something like this for so long. Do we let our hopes get up only to have them dashed back to the ground in a week or two? We have seen this before and then the bottom falls out. The rollercoaster ride was getting more difficult and although Becky was going to get a two-month break, we were having a hard time understanding what had just happened. It was still one of the most troubling moments in the journey.

It was the first time I felt a little anger. I don't know, maybe I was losing it. The whole fight was becoming a battle of unknowns and confusion, but I'm sure you are reading along thinking this looks like the break we were looking for. Yes, we were glad for the break, but what about that spot?

What about that spot?

We got back to town late and just crashed in our bed. We were both tired. Physically tired, emotionally tired, and I think for the first time even a little spiritually tired. We were going to have to setup another appointment with a new doctor, but who do we get? We don't know any of those urology people. Ugh! I didn't want to do it, but you have to keep going.

This battle was starting to get the best of me. You get one thing figured out, and one more thing jumps up in front of you. This kidney thing was just one more issue we weren't expecting and now we have to fight it too. Anyone would grow weary. I was being honest with Becky that evening. I have never been one to "put on the face" and keep things hidden. There are times when all you can do is cry out to God. The Bible is full of stories of people doing this. I am not talking about complaining. I believe those are vastly different things. Complaining is not resting in God. Complaining is being selfish in midst of the mess.

My God, my God, why have you forsaken me?
Why are you so far from helping me, from the words of my
groaning?

O my God, I cry by day, but you do not answer;
and by night, but find no rest.

There are moments in any great struggle when we come to the end of our personal skills and strength. I believe in these times God is waiting. When Jesus was in the garden praying, that prayer was not a "quick fix" prayer. It was the words of a struggling man who fully understood what was ahead. The weight of the moment was too much, even for the Son of God. Jesus was weary of the battle, and looking ahead didn't seem all that inviting to him. His prayer is crying out to his Father. The Father would speak, and the angels would come. That's what Becky and I needed...some angels.

Abbie would write:

Here is an update on Becky Teel. She and Clyde Teel
returned from Mayo last night. On Monday they met with
the oncologist. Mom's C19 marker was down in the 600s,
but that was not important to the oncologist. (We took a
little heart in it. :-D) On Tuesday, they tried to do a biopsy,
but that was not important to the oncologist. (We took a
little heart in it. :-D) They tried to do a biopsy, but the
mass is in a spot that they cannot get to. A PET scan was
done on Wednesday. The mass is very small. Next steps...
Mom will take 8 weeks off of chemo to get her blood and
body back to "healthy" levels before they make the
decision of what's next in chemo-world. They will do
another PET scan at that time and then we will look at
decisions that need to be made.
Unfortunately, her kidneys are not working terribly well,
in accordance with some very high blood pressure. She
has an appointment next week with a specialist in town to
figure that out. Hopefully being off the chemo will help the
kidney situation, but we are requesting prayer for that.
So, prayer for kidneys to work and cancer to stay at bay,

The rest of the world didn't take a break and we didn't either. We continued to do things that were "fun." You can't let life get you down. Dalton and I were doing some music things that spring. We would go and do a little two-man bluegrass program at some of the local hangouts. For the few minutes we were doing that, life was about playing instruments and singing old songs, not cancer. Dalton would often stop over to our house and the two of us would sit and "jam." When Becky felt good enough she would reach over from her chair and play a little bass with us. It was a healing time. There were lots of times in the middle of the day that I would run home to see how she was doing and ask her if she wanted to play a few songs. We played often at first, but it was getting harder for her to concentrate now. She would get tired quickly and have to stop.

Something was not right.

Becky would write very little during these first few months of the year. She was tired and hurting most of the time. Usually she would repost things from Abbie's blog and make brief comments. Here are a few of them to read. You'll see Becky's heart.

Waiting on God...... Keep me strong in the waiting.

God has blessed me with wonderfully deep children!

I'm having coffee with Jesus this morning.

Remembering who I am in God..... A whole new way to pray !

My only job is to love Jesus!!

Jesus is in heaven praying for me! What a beautiful thought!

God is on my side!

Yes, Jesus, stay close so your peace can reign in me!

What is your plan to get into heaven?
Open my eyes to see everywhere you are working my God.

She was going to take two months off from the chem. She was so hoping during that time that she would get back some of her lost strength, but that wasn't happening. We had made the appointment with the kidney doctor who put Becky on some meds and a carefully regimented plan to get things working again. That part of the journey almost seems like a diversion from the raging battle that was still ahead. Even Dr. M. wasn't that concerned with the kidneys. He had been monitoring that for several months so he was aware of that problem all along. When we had gotten back from Mayo we did a follow up with him. He was fine with our taking the two months off, but I always wonder what he was thinking. I never asked.

Easter was coming.

Easter is the day we Christians celebrate the resurrected life. It is the day we wave the banner of hope to the world. We say the grave didn't win. The cross went from a seemingly meaningless tragedy to a triumph of redemption. Jesus is alive. Throughout all these months I had been talking about the power of the risen Christ. On Palm Sunday I talked about God not being a "Fixer," but a "Redeemer."

I don't want to get all preachy here, but I had learned so much over the course of these many months. I learned deep things about myself about who God was "in the valley." It had been the most powerful spiritual experiences of my life to this point. I felt empowered to share what I was learning. The road Becky was traveling had opened the eyes, ears, and hearts of so many people that all I had to do was speak what my heart was feeling and the words seemed to penetrate. The ground had become fertile. We knew it was her struggle that was making that possible. God was taking what was tragic and making it a blessing to many. It was obvious God was working, but this was not a place anyone ever wants to walk.

That paradox or tension, whatever you want to call it, was a troubling part of the story, but evident to us. I wish I could express this with more eloquent words, but words fail me.

April was the second month of being off chemo and still Becky was *not* getting better. We were good at knowing what chemo sick was all about, but this sick was different. We talked about waiting for the two months to pass, but it seemed like the best thing to do now was call Dr. M. because something was not right. I made an appointment with Dr. M. He suggested we come right away.

We drove over to the clinic and waited to see him. When Dr. M. came into the room I think he could see immediately what I was seeing. She was very tired and starting to complain of some pain in her lower back. She had lost more weight and now that weight loss was getting *very* noticeable. I could hear the concern in his voice this time. He ordered a scan and some test to be done right away.

We would have the tests on Maundy Thursday and get the results back on Good Friday. Amazing timing! Is that not crazy?

Our church always has a powerful Maundy Thursday service. Maundy Thursday is the day set aside in the church calendar for recognizing the night when Jesus washed the disciples' feet. It is the observance of the last supper. It had been a long tradition at Community and a very special time to gather the church together. It was a packed house that night. I explained what had happened earlier in the day, and I told them we would be getting the results of the scan the next day. By now the church was fully engaged in this battle. They had lived through the same ups and downs. They had experienced all of that with us and they had their own lives too. Everyone does.

Becky and I drove separate cars to the clinic on Good Friday. We arrived there almost at the same time…walked in together…and back to the little room to wait. Dr. M. came in and sat in his usual place. He went to the computer and began to open the file. I was numb. I didn't really know what to expect. Neither of us did. We had talked this over so many times before to predict how it would go. Most of the time we missed, so, why try?

Dr. M. who is always right to the point started reading the report out loud. It reminded me so much of the first diagnosis as I sat there listening to those medical terms going by one by one. He turned around to both of us and in a steady voice he said, "Becky, the cancer is back. It has found its way into the lining that surrounds your stomach. There is a good chance this is where it has always been. We just couldn't see it."

Immediately it made sense to me. This would explain why we could never find a tumor. Those numbers would go up, and we would do a scan. The scan would come back clear, and that was always so aggravating. How could those numbers be so high and yet nothing would show on the scans? Well, now we knew. There *was* something going on. The lining now was thick enough to finally show up on the scan.

Dr. M. went on to say, "The scan was like looking through a foggy glass."

My heart was sinking. Dr. M. said Becky could do another round of chemo, but this time the chemo would be very powerful. He wasn't sure her body could handle it considering the state of her health at this point.

"What would be the gain?" Becky asked.

"It would give you a little more time, Becky," he said.

Dr. M. never used the word terminal. He never once said that word, but we knew what was coming. The conversation changed to quality of life matters. There was no more "fix it." We were all discussing this as if we were talking about the next car we might purchase or if we liked whole wheat or rye bread. I don't think it had really hit us yet.

> I don't think it had really hit us yet.

He said he would give us the weekend to think it all over. We could come on Monday and let him know what we had decided. It was our choice. He told her she had done well and that she was *his* patient. He was going to take good care of her no matter what we decided. He walked out of the room and we followed behind him. There were nurses there. They all knew. There were tears in their eyes. It was starting to hit home. The landscape had just changed again.

Jesus be near because this is really hard.

We walked out of that clinic to go home. I decided to call Liz and Becky was going to call Abbie and Dalton. It was such a sick feeling. I drove home alone. It felt like my mind was going a thousand miles an hour, yet it was standing still at the same time. Becky had gone through so much over this past year and half and now it comes to this. *What will she do?* I had a feeling I knew what she would decide because we had talked about this very thing many times before. The kids came over to spend the rest of the day with us. Later that day Abbie would write:

> *Update on Becky Teel: Mom had a PET scan done yesterday, a little earlier than planned, due to her not feeling well at all. She has been fighting very nasty back pain and her stomach has been feeling awful. With that the scan revealed why she was feeling so icky. The cancer has spread. She is taking some medication to manage the pain. They will meet with the oncologist again on Monday to talk about what's next.*
>
> *I honestly have no words. We spent the day as a family, crying, laughing, and just being for a bit. This is a tough battle and a really tough place to be in. However, we know who wins. We know who holds tomorrow. We know that God is big enough to handle all of this. We have someone bigger than our circumstance. As Dad said last night, God is a redeemer, not a fixer. This is ringing true for us today. Oh, we still hope for a "fix," but, no matter the outcome, we know she is redeemed.*
>
> *So for Easter weekend, hug your loved ones tightly, share words of truth and love, and be sure you meet the Redeemer, Jesus Christ. His death was not in vain. We are not defeated because he has been resurrected. We have Jesus and in him is the victory! Sunday is coming!!!!*

On Saturday morning I would write:

> *An update on Becky*
> *I am sitting in my office this morning preparing a word for the people in the morning. Tomorrow is Easter Sunday. The girls have already written an update for their mom… they share amazing words. If you haven't read those, I would encourage you to do that.*

Becky received some hard news yesterday. We had been noticing a change in her condition over the last several days and so with that came a doctor recommendation to do a scan and see what we might find. On Good Friday we got the results. The cancer is growing and spreading. Monday morning we go in to discuss just how we will proceed. Some tougher chemo to slow this down...or just stop. Neither option has much appeal, but it is all there is now. We are people of hope who know and believe at any point a miracle could come. We press on.

So faced with this news, what will this preacher say tomorrow to these church folks who are coming for an Easter Sunday celebration? I know one thing. I will be as real as I can be. I will share what I always share...I will offer them an opportunity to not just talk about the resurrection, but to live in it! I have no problem saying this has been hard, painful, wearisome, scary, and more than I can handle on my own, but I'm not living in a place of paralyzing fear of an unknown tomorrow. I have a risen Jesus in my life...He carries me now. His presence sustains me...I am living in "resurrection."

I am truly blessed with so many people who are so important to me. So many of you who give so much. It means everything now. We have great kids...with deep hearts...who bring such inner strength to the journey. And...We're prayed up!
Thanks everyone
Have A Blessed Easter

Easter Sunday 2014 - Living In Resurrection

The message on Easter Sunday was titled "Living In Resurrection." The message was about defeating death and living our lives a *place* called Resurrection. It is a mindset we can have. A "heart" set if you will. It is walking *through* the valley of the shadow of death and not around it. It is like looking the greatest fear in our lives straight in the eye and shouting the words, "I win!"

We as a family are not the kind of people who give up when life gets heavy. I want everyone to understand that as you read this. There are voices in our Christian world who seem to suggest that if we keep a good strong attitude and proclaim victory, then God will make everything come to pass just like you ask. I don't want to poke at that kind of thinking with a sharp stick, but I don't see that always play out. I have seen healing like that, I have, but I have also seen things just fall apart no matter what they do. If getting is about earning, then Becky's cancer should have been gone. If it is about praying, then Becky's cancer should have been taken away. That's all I will say about this now. I'll speak to that later, at the end of the story.

Abbie's blog that week would have this entry:

Wednesday, April 30, 2014
Peace Within

Philippians 4:6-7 Do not be anxious about anything, but in everything, by prayer and petition, with thanksgiving, present your requests to God. And the peace of God, which transcends all understanding, will guard your hearts and your minds in Christ Jesus.

We think that the answers to prayer can only be yes or no. I've even heard an interpretation of God's answers to prayer as "yes" and "wait a while". That doesn't seem quite right to me either. As I read this verse, it makes me think that the answer to prayer is completely irrelevant. Paul says "present your requests to God" and then his very next statement is, "And the peace of God...will guard your hearts and minds." Paul says nothing about the answer to the prayer, not 'And He will give you all of your requests' or 'pray harder and God will do as you ask.' No. Paul's statement is simply paraphrased, talk to God about what you desire and He will give you peace in Christ Jesus. Don't pray to get an answer. Pray to receive peace within.

After church that Easter Sunday the family went home ,which was a little unusual for us because we usually go out to eat. It was our Sunday tradition. We had done it for

106

years. It was a chance for the whole family to unpack the morning's news and talk about the message or the music. I guess you might say it was our chance to talk "Jesus stuff" for few minutes. Usually there is lots of laughter because Dalton would be slinging some of that good ol' southern humor at us. Those Sunday lunches were some of the best times we shared together. But on this day it seemed right to go home (to our house), and prepare our own meal. After all, it was Easter.

We were sitting around the living room getting ready for lunch. I don't remember what we were having. That didn't matter. Becky was standing by a plant stand next to the clock while we talked about the morning's events. I had brought home a couple of the flower arrangements from the morning's celebration, and I had set one on that plant stand. Becky was standing there admiring those flowers. She loved flowers!

Now, I never take pictures. Oh, I might now and then, but I am not the kind of guy who runs around with my phone making folks line up and smile. It's just not me. I am usually not even thinking about the camera on my phone. As a matter of fact, I have missed some great photos because of that very thing. As she stood there next to those flowers, without a second thought I said, "I'll take a picture. Smile."

Smile? Clyde is going to take a picture?

It would be the last photo we took of Becky.

We had a good day that day. One of the best Easters I can remember, but not the easiest. I am sure you can understand. Monday was going to be the day that Becky would make her big decision. We had told the church family that morning that Monday was the day she was going to make her decision, but I already knew what she was going to do. She was so worn down from this mess and she was tired of being sick. She was thinking maybe if she didn't do this chemo thing that maybe she might gain some quality time. She wasn't at all interested in just getting more time. She had been sick for so long, a year and a half now of being sick. If you have been reading this story you are no doubt sick of it as well. She was done with all that.

I want you to know that our family was not naive. We all knew too well that without an amazing miracle from God, beyond anything we had ever experienced before, we were going to lose her. Life was very real for us during those last days and we were very aware of what Becky was facing.

....

Another Monday

Monday morning we drove over to the clinic, together this time. There were some tears on the way over as we drove. We had talked and talked the night before about the journey we all had gone through. She was very tired and getting very weak. She was deeply cancer sick now and you could see it. We walked in. Same routine. Now you know it too. Back to that little room. We only sat there together for a short time and the door opened. Dr. M. came in and sat down on his little stool with the wheels. There was no need to look at the computer; he just asked the question. "Well, what did you decide?"

Becky looked at him and with her calm voice she said, "I don't want to do any more medicine."

"I understand," he said.

They both sat there face to face and talked about a few medical things. My mind was spinning. I was simply wondering what was next. Then Becky did one of the most amazing things. She spoke to him in that same calm, yet now slightly cracking, voice and said, "Dr. M., I just want you know that you did a great job. And if I had to do it over again, I would still choose you."

I knew she meant it. Every single word!

I knew she meant it. Every single word!

He just sat there. Not saying a word. His face flushed a bit. He politely said something back to her, but I can't remember his words. At that moment, no matter what he said, it wasn't going to top what she said to him.

Becky never had any anger...ever. Even now being confronted with what was possibly coming, she was able to look him in the eye and tell him exactly how she felt. I sat there nodding. I couldn't speak. She owned the moment. I look back now and I marvel at her courage. Becky never took any credit for any of that extra strength she would sometimes display. She was a girl trusting in God to take her through this, and He was!

We got up to leave and said goodbye to Dr. M. Becky would not see him again. It was their last moment together. Powerful! We walked out of the room together one last time. The staff at the clinic told us we really needed to think about hospice care right away. As a pastor I had seen this with other families and it is the right way to go. Hospice can do so much for you by answering questions and setting up a plan for you. It gives such peace of mind knowing that you don't have to make a decision yourself in tough moments. They are right there and they are wonderful people. We made an appointment to meet with them. It was a new day again.

Chapter IX
Living At The End

Hospice

We made an appointment to meet with the hospice staff the following week. I set up the appointment so our whole family could be there because it seemed right that we all go. The meeting was going to be in the new cancer center at the Avera medical center in Sioux Falls. It was a beautiful new building which helped our hearts a little I think. The setting is very comforting. We all arrived and took the elevator up to the second floor where we were greeted by a receptionist telling us to have a seat. The hospice team would be right out to meet with us. We didn't have to wait long. One of the hospice reps came out to greet us and take us back to a small conference room. We found our place around the large table in the center of the room, and the staff joined us. There was a pharmacist, a counselor, a medical doctor and a chaplain as a part of this team of people who spoke to us about all the resources we would have during this part of our journey. We all shared very openly about Becky's journey thus far, and they answered questions we had. It was a great meeting. We learned a lot and were given all the information on how to get things moving.

The plan would start with a home-care team who would be stopping by the house a few times during the week. There was also a little education for us in how to do what was coming. There were phone numbers, contacts, and schedules, all very well planned out and wonderfully efficient. I was so thankful for choosing hospice care. I had never been down this path before. None of us had. There is no learning manual on this one. You do it one day at a time, and to be very honest, the journey will lead you. You don't lead it.

The hospice folks said (seriously, they did!) that we were the most joyful family they had ever seen in that room. Becky talked much more than usual that day. I shared, and the kids did too. In each of our stories there were moments of laughter, humor, moments of tears, and a deep sense of being uplifted through Becky's long fight. It's how we had lived every moment of the journey. Evidently, our joy was showing on the outside as well. They were such encouraging people. It was a good choice.

We drove home ready for what was ahead, at least as ready as we could be. Becky, as I said earlier, was hoping things would level off a little. She would have no chemo now for several weeks and she was really hoping her body might begin to respond in a more positive direction. Sadly, that wasn't going to happen. That was so very disappointing for her.

We were given phone numbers to call and steps of action to take when things started to change. There was a home visit a couple times a week by a nurse who would help us monitor all of the things that were coming at us. I am writing with my mind nearly in a blur as I try to remember the experiences of those last days with Becky. It was almost more than I could handle, looking back on it now, but I want to do my very best to describe it for you. There was no other time like this in our lives. The hours Becky and I would share together would become almost *holy*. Each conversation took on a new level of intimacy. Even the smallest detail became the richest blessing. Everything matters!

Our first challenge was controlling the pain. I am not sure how much to share, so I'll just ramble for a bit. They have great pain meds for this "mess" and for the most part, we were able to keep things under control. The best advice was stay ahead of the game and don't get behind, but to do that means you have to keep a steady hand on the wheel. Your attention has to be focused all the time on each medication. Every day would be a challenge to get it all right. I could call anytime for advice, and I did. The pain Becky was experiencing was mostly in her lower back and it could get very nasty if we let it go too long.

Once you have a handle on the pain meds, then a second problem begins to unfold. Pain meds at any level can effect your lower intestinal track. You get constipated, to put it bluntly, as if there is any other way to say it. You have to constantly be adjusting all those bowel meds as well. I never knew there were so many things the world of medicine had to offer to get everything "going." There are low level, medium level, and, yes, even a level I would call the "oh my goodness" level. I am writing this with a smile now because you have to keep a certain level of humor or it would drive you crazy. You would be angry the rest of your life if you didn't find a way to wade through the muck. (No pun intended.) I can't begin to explain how many hours we both spent working on pain or working on…well, you know what

111

I mean. Our conversations seemed to be me asking her which meds she took and when was the last time she went potty! Ugh!

And then, to add another piece to this changing puzzle, we were trying to keep blood platelet levels high. They would drop and we would have to do transfusions. We had those issues before, but I didn't even talk about that until now because I didn't want to overwhelm you as you read through the story.

Fluids, oh yes, there was the fluid issue. If you remember back earlier I would take Becky into the clinic to *give* her fluid because she was dehydrated. Well now...she was holding too much water so we would make several trips to the clinic to remove that excess water from her tummy. This procedure was not complicated, but it was not the most pleasant for her. It hurt! We finally had a drain installed so she wouldn't have to be poked each time. This drain will come up later in the story.

The emotional pull of all this medical responsibility, together with the fact that life was still going on around us, became very challenging. The world doesn't go on hold just because we have cancer going on in our lives. The church was going great! Again, I say one of the most amazing parts of this story was just how well things were going on around us, then in this one place, this very significant place, it was just a mess. Each day there was a little change. I don't know how many times Becky and I would sit and talk about our lives, our kids, this cancer, her fears, and our courage. I would ask her, "What have you learned Becky? Tell me what this is like."

Even at this point in the journey she couldn't believe it was going to take her life. I could fill an entire book with just the conversations we had together during the last days. We talked a lot. Sometimes it was simple moments of sharing about our lives. And sometimes the moments were so deep and so...sad.

There are some conversations I will never forget because they changed me so deeply. She was holding on for an amazing miracle. There were a couple of days when she actually started feeling a little better. The pain eased a little there for a time and she was able to get out and enjoy life. She would call her good friend, Linda. They would talk or Linda would come over and they would have some good quality time together. Normal, or at least close to normal.

Becky started telling me that she was feeling pretty good and maybe this was going to change. She was feeling better.

Becky would write:

> *It's been a pretty good day. God gave me energy to have coffee with a dear friend. Now it's more resting time, but I'm resting in His arms, so that is really good!!*

Then one evening the pain got a little out of hand and her tummy wasn't working. She got very sick and the reality of what was going on really began to hit her. She started crying out loud. She had not cried like this before. This was new. I felt so helpless. She just walked over to the bed and fell back.

"I'm dying. I'm dying." she sobbed.

I had no words. What do you say to someone in that moment? I doubt if any lecture or sermon on spiritual growth could make any difference for what was happening at that moment. It was the first

> **"I'm dying. I'm dying." she sobbed.**

time I cried in front of her. Oh, I would frequently get misty eyed about things. I would even have moments when I couldn't speak or my speech would become shaky, but this time I couldn't hold back. We laid on the bed together… crying. There were 40 years of memories behind us. I was so sad for her. This long journey was coming to an end and this was not what we wanted, but we had no way to stop what was coming.

Jesus be near. This is hard.

The days continued to pass one by one. Our church family was so good to us during this difficult time. I never once had to remind them not to rush in. This is a fairly large church and they could have so easily overwhelmed us with visits and food, but they didn't. We would get cards by the basket full, but they kept a perfectly healthy distance. It was as if they knew this was our time to walk together. I am so blessed. I had close friends that I would talk to. Some of them were like angels attending. I know I could have never walked that path without them. I will write more about all this later. We were walking in that valley now. Never alone. Not once. Not ever. God was so present, at times nearly overwhelming. T he girls were seeing that too.

On May 15th Liz wrote:

Friends, I feel like it might be good to give an update on my mom, Becky Teel.
You may remember from my Easter weekend post that we found out Mom's cancer had spread, and we were going to have to make decisions about what to do next. After much prayer, talking, thinking, prayer, and more prayer, Mom decided, along with the full support of our family, that she didn't want to do the next nasty level of chemo. Quality of life is much more important to her than quantity of days, and after fighting pancreatic cancer for 1 year and 9 months, she (and we) fully understand what it means to have quality of life as opposed to chemo sick days.

So for a couple of weeks now, Mom has been doing Home Hospice care. For those of you who don't know, hospice care is so much more than immediate end of life care. If you enter the hospice program early enough, the wonderful nurses and doctors to whom you are assigned get the chance to meet their patients and really get to know them, which translates to even better care for them. Mom's hospice nurses have been phenomenal. They help with meds, they are available anytime, day or night, to come to the house if needed, they answer questions and offer support, and even occasionally make suggestions about how to give her even better care. We find hospice care to be a miracle in itself, and we are deeply grateful for it.

This is an unexplainable place to be. My whole family has found God to be immensely big in this season. We are deeply sad and shed many tears over what's happening, but we truly have God's peace that passes understanding. We are living in the reality of today in this broken world, but we are living here with the power of the eternal resurrection available to us every single moment! This power of God, because of Jesus' death, and through the Holy Spirit, is sustaining and gives us exactly what we need to continue on each day. I praise Him for that!

Mom has good days and bad days. Good moments and bad moments. And we just keep pressing on. We continue to ask God for a miracle, but above that, we ask God to accomplish His will because only He knows what the best outcome is for this situation. We absolutely trust Him and His will. Again, I believe we are only able to say that because He has given us His peace that passes understanding. WE are not strong in this. WE are WEAK! But when we are weak, HE is strong in us. What an amazing God we serve!

So dear friends, we'd love continued prayers for good pain management, for continued peace that passes understanding, for strength and grace for each day, even for a healing miracle, but above all, for God's good will to be accomplished through this trial, for His glory. That might sound cheesy, but it is really the truth of how my family feels, and it's how we are praying.

As one of my good friends commented, "A 'like' on this status means that we are standing with the Teels." So yes; we know if you "like" my status, you are not liking what's happening. You are sending your love and support like you've done for 21 months now. You all have been absolutely amazing! Thank you for the countless prayers, hugs, kind words, letters, and support you've given to my family. You have been Jesus' hands and feet to us, and it has been beautiful!

And now to close...Romans 8:37-39 "No, in all these these we are more than conquerors through Him who loved us. For I am convinced that neither death nor life, neither angels nor demons, neither the present nor the future, nor any powers, neither height nor depth, nor anything else in all creation, will be able to separate us from the love of God that is in Christ Jesus our Lord." Amen!

Becky would have people stop by. Her sisters would drive over and spend time with her. Becky had lost a sister to cancer a few years before which was another sad time for her family. The Mayer sisters were close. They spent as much time as they could just doing fun things. They were scattered around the country so it wasn't always easy for them to get together, but when they did it was always a good time for them. For the ones who lived close to us, they would stop over to see her. Becky was now starting to spend a lot of time in bed. I can remember one day when Becky's oldest sister Karen was back in the room with her. I was in the kitchen doing something and Karen was back there reading scripture and sharing some stories about people who had *won* their battle with cancer.

I heard Becky say, "Karen, I don't want to hear those stories anymore. Can we just talk?"

Becky just needed to spend time with her sister. The victory stories didn't matter anymore. I asked her about that conversation later and Becky had plenty to say. I will share more about this later, but for now let me just say I think we forget how important "being there" is for people. I find that too often people are paralyzed in difficult moments because they never know what to say. Trust me, your presence has a power far beyond your words. Be quiet if you want. Don't say anything, and let God fill the silence.

There were other friends who would stop by from time to time. I remember when her friend Vickie came by. Vickie had taken Becky's place at Trail Ridge. She was a sweet lady who just wanted to see Becky. Vickie had called for an "appointment" which I thought was so cute, at least that's how Becky would later refer to it. She spent one afternoon just being by her bedside on one of Becky's tired days. They were talking about all kinds of things. Much of the conversation was Vickie telling Becky how much she admired her life and how great a friend Becky had been. At one point in the conversation Vickie asked Becky a question that really caught my attention. She asked, "Becky, is there anything you wish you could have done. Anything you didn't get to do?"

My ears perked up because I realized what a great question that really was. Why hadn't I asked that? I asked dozens of other questions, but not that one. It was quiet for only a moment and Becky responded, "No, not one thing."

How many people can say that?

Really, Becky, not one thing?

She would tell people she only wished she could see the new church wing "in action." She didn't want to leave her family. She would tell her close friend, who later shared with me, that she worried about me when she was gone and how different my life would be, the new challenges I would face. She was going to miss playing with the family band and sharing times we spent doing fun things together. But beyond that she would miss nothing. That was so Becky!

Food had always been an issue in her cancer battle I am sure you remember all of that from before. I would come home and ask her what she would like for lunch. Most of the time nothing really sounded good to her. It wasn't like I had any amazing recipes, but I was getting pretty good at this kitchen work. I would try to fix something that I thought would work for her tummy. She would come walking slowly out of the bedroom, sit down with me, and pick away at something. Sometimes she would get a little eaten maybe a few swallows of rice and drink a little of one of those tasty energy drinks. She might even have a bite or two of fruit. I remember her sitting there staring at the food in front of her on a rough day. I'm not sure what we were having, but she started crying. It was a sad cry.

"I can't do it," she said. "I'm sorry."

"It's okay, you don't have to," I told her. I didn't like this place. The road was too painful now. My heart was downcast.

Psalm 42:9-11

I say to God, my rock,
  "Why have you forgotten me?
Why must I walk about mournfully
  because the enemy oppresses me?"

As with a deadly wound in my body,
  my adversaries taunt me,
while they say to me continually,
  "Where is your God?"

Why are you cast down, O my soul,
  and why are you disquieted within me?
Hope in God; for I shall again praise him,
  my help and my God.

Everything was changing.

She wanted to go out to the church and look at the new wing. We had finished the wing and the dedication service was the Sunday before. Becky did get to go to that, but she had spent most of that morning in my office sleeping. She just couldn't do it all, but she wanted to have enough energy to be there for the dedication. So later that week she asked if we could go out there again. I took her out to the church and we drove around to the back door so that we could just have a little time alone. We got out and went in through the back door. She walked in and started looking at all the rooms in the new wing. It would be her last time there.

We moved slowly around to each room and made little comments as we went. She had only a few questions about some of the rooms. She loved the little chairs and those little toys in the new part of the nursery wing. She would go along and touch things. I had never seen her do that before. It was as if she was trying to get a "feel" for everything…soaking it all up. She walked around the rest of the building too all of which she had seen before, but just one more time. It was a holy time. I just stood and watched.

We had given our lives to this place for 16 years. Nearly every conversation our family had was around the people and ministry of this place we call Community. We had made this decision together to do this ministry calling. Now that was changing. We walked through the big room, at least that's what I call it. It is the worship center. She walked right down the center aisle and up to front and turned to her right. She walked over to her music stand…her spot. It would be the last time. She turned and said, "I'm getting tired."

She cried tears, and it took everything I had to keep it together. The room was full.

Last things are hard. You don't fully appreciate it at the time, but looking back now it really hits you. There will be more of these moments and I want to share those with you. Every single second that goes by is a gift. I often tell people now, "When you have a good day, celebrate that to the fullest!" Our days matter more than you can ever know, and when they are gone, they are gone. And gone is *gone*.

Last Things

I was doing a little house cleaning and picking up a few things because Becky's friend, Donna, was coming over to give Becky a pedicure. Donna was another of those special friends Becky had made over the years. Donna was a hairdresser too and she and Becky had worked together for a number of years.

Becky wrote about the day:

> *Nice visit... Great pedicure.... Wonderful time... With a good friend yesterday. Enjoying the small things in life. One day at a time.*

As I was cleaning, Becky had her little bass amp and her bass guitar sitting in the corner of the living room. She just left it there because in our house instruments are sitting everywhere...perfect! Instruments are like pieces of furniture to us. You never know when you may get the urge to pick one up and start playing so you need to have it close by. I was going around doing a little cleaning up and I decided to put that bass away in its case. Becky hadn't played it for a number of days, and I, without much thought, made a decision to find the case and put it away. Simple, right? Donna came over and they had a great time with Donna fussing over Becky's feet. Later that evening, Becky had some tears going again, and whenever I would see tears I would say something like, "Oh, we have tears. Talk to me." She would always have something to share.

That evening she looked up and said, "I see you put my bass away."

Then it hit me. "Oh no...I'm so sorry, I didn't mean..." I tried to explain.

"It's okay," she said. "I'm probably not going to play it again."

I felt so bad. I didn't mean to have her think that way, but her heart was in a new place. She was holding on to every moment...*every moment.*

Becky was our hairdresser. I hadn't had another hand on my head in over 40 years. Every haircut was hers. Liz and Abbie too, Mom always did their hair. There was coming a day now when each of us, including Dalton, was going to get the *last* haircut. I can't begin to share what that was like for us. That moment was off the charts when it comes to what goes through your mind and heart. We have a wonderful picture of Liz getting her last haircut. Becky was doing hair right up to the very end. She would get out of bed if needed and tell us she could do it one more time. She would be so tired, but she wanted to do it. I can't imagine what she must have been thinking during those times. She had been cutting those girls' hair their entire life. They would run down to the shop on Main in Burke, grab a pop out of the pop machine, and jump in chair. Mom was going to fix 'em up! They got perms, colors, and anything else you have done to hair. Who knows how much money we saved.

Abbie's last hair day was the most amazing. Abbie is a brunette, (sorry Abbie, it's out now) but as a little girl she was white blonde! She preferred that blonde color so for years Becky would do it blonde. Becky had Abbie's coloring down to a fine art. The process was pretty involved to get it just right. Becky could nail it every time, but it was hard work. To complicate matters, Abbie keeps her hair very short. I'm not a hair expert, but I've been told blonde and short is a nasty combination.

Becky wanted to do it one more time. The two of them set about the task of coloring and cutting. Becky was getting so tired, but she was determined to do it. At one point Becky was too tired to stand so she sat in the chair and Abbie moved to the floor. There they were, mom and daughter sharing this moment together. They had done this dozens of times before, but this one was different...the last time. Whatever it was going to take, Becky was going to get it done...this one last time. They did it together! It was perfect. We build our lives around moments like this. Those kind of moments have a value greater than all the riches money could ever buy. Moments shared by a mom and her daughter. Words fail me to describe it. It is something I will never forget.

Becky would write:

> *Pretty good day over all. God has been good. One day at a time.*

Becky couldn't go to church anymore. We had spent years going through our usual routine on Sunday morning. We would get up early and drive out to the new site. We would arrive usually before the sunrise. I would do my duties unlocking the doors and setting up all the "techy" things. Becky would get the coffee bar going and then she would sit at a table in the lobby and wait for our first "guests" to arrive. She was like the church homemaker waiting for her friends to come for a little morning coffee time. I would join her there for a few minutes and wait as the sun would come streaming through the windows. It was a routine we knew like the backs of our hands.

Our first service on Sunday was a small group of mostly older folks who would arrive in nearly the same order each week. Usually Walt and Carol would come first, then Hank and Clazina...maybe Dorland and Shirley, then Alvin and Dolly...you get the picture.

But now, in these last days, I was going alone. Sundays were very different.

Her friend Linda would come over to the house to watch the service with Becky on the new live stream. Linda was a little more "techy" than Becky so together they made a good team. Linda shared Becky's last church service on the web. I don't know if Linda has thought about that, but I have. I had shared hundreds of Sunday mornings with Becky, but I didn't get to share the last one. I got home that day, and Linda laughed because they had quite a struggle getting that "stupid live-stream" to work. Becky was tired. Linda gave her a hug and off she went.

When Sunday evening came there were lots of issues to deal with. She was getting so tired and very sick. She was now starting to have difficulty keeping all her thoughts together and that was bothering me a bit. I was not angry or anything like that, I was just a bit unsettled because this was something new again and something I really hadn't prepared for.

I wasn't sure how the "end" would come. I thought she would just get more tired and then that would be all, but that was not how this was going to go at all. I got her ready for bed that night and, of course, there were lots of other things going on. I don't need to go through any of that here because at this point in the story you probably have some idea anyway. Becky felt so bad for me. I didn't care what it was going to take. I was going to do it. You don't really know what you are capable of until you are there. I didn't even think about it. I just did it. I don't want to sound like a hero because I am not. Things were getting tough and I was calling the hospice nurse often. She was stopping a couple of times each *day* to check on Becky.

She went to bed that Sunday night and went right to sleep. The one blessing for Becky on this journey was the way she could sleep. That girl could sleep! So many people say that sleeping was something they couldn't do. Well, she could.

She would write:

> *Yes, Father , you are the great healer!! Your will be done! I love you!*

Followed by:

> *I have been blessed with flowers!! I love them!*

These would be her last words on social media. God indeed was everywhere!

Chapter X
Jesus Knows What To Do.

Another Monday

Monday morning I was going to be at a meeting, so I laid all the pills out for her on the countertop in the kitchen. I checked with her while she was in bed to see how she was doing. She said she was tired of course, but not feeling any pain. I told her I had laid everything out on the counter for her morning regimen of pills just like always. Everything seemed like it was going to be just another day. I also knew the hospice nurse would be coming around 9am to check, but just to be on the safe side I had asked Dalton if he would come by and check on her. I'm glad I did. He had been so good during all of this. I could write one entire chapter just on Dalton's amazing spirit during this trying time. He was such a breath of fresh air on so many occasions throughout this journey. I knew he would be good with her. Becky loved Dalton. So off I went for my day. I was only a few minutes from the house when my phone rang. It was Becky, and in this rather shaky voice she said,"Clyde, I can't figure out the pills."

I patiently told her how to do it.

"Do I take them all?" she asked.

"Yes, take them all, okay?" I replied.

"Okay." "When are you coming home?" she asked with an almost childlike voice.

I could tell something was wrong, but I had seen so much already. Was this something different? I was trying to reassure her that everything was going to be okay, but my confidence was beginning to fade. I was just about to turn around when she said the hospice nurse had arrived. Her voice lifted a bit and I could hear the nurse talking to her in the background. "Okay, she's here now," Becky said. "It's fine." I said goodbye.

Something seemed different, but it was early in the day. Sometimes in the morning she was tired and seemed to get better as the day moved along. The nurse was there and I knew if something had changed the nurse would call. My confidence was back. Everything would be okay, at least for now. I got through my meeting and was driving home later in the day. I decided to call Liz and see how things were going because I knew she had stopped over to see her mom.

Liz answered, "Are you coming home?"

"Yes, I'll be there shortly. Why?" I asked.

"Something is wrong with Mom," Liz said.

Liz went on to explain that Mom was walking around the house "needing to get something done." Dalton and Liz had tried to get her to lie down, but Becky would get right back up and start walking around the house looking for that "something" that needed to be done. I felt sick for the kids. They were all there now, Abbie too, trying to get this situation under control. I got there as fast as I could and hurried into the house. The kids were sitting there, all three of them lined up on the couch in the living room. I came up the stairs and one of them said, "There is something wrong with Mom."

They all looked very concerned, even a bit confused by what had been going on, but I could also see that they were sure glad I was there. I went right back to the bedroom to check on Becky. As I moved down the hallway I could hear her moving around. Becky was just getting out of bed as I came into the room and she looked at me with a confused kind of look. It is hard to describe how she looked, but it was different. Something *was* wrong.

"I don't know what to do," she said in a soft, feeble voice. And then she said it again, "I don't know what to do."

I tried to talk some sense into her and asked, "What is it you're supposed to do?"

"I don't know," she said, "I don't know what to do."

I could tell she was anxious about something and she needed to move. So I took her by the hand and we walked out into the hallway to the living room as if we had some purpose, which neither of us knew. We walked and walked and she kept saying that little phrase over and over. I finally got her back in bed and told her she was just tired. I tried to convince her there wasn't anything to do, and I went back out to the living room. I told the kids, "Why don't you guys go home now. I think Mom and I need to do this. Okay?"

They were fine with that. They didn't know what to do either. This was all coming at them so fast and none of us were expecting this kind of change. They got their stuff and told me if I needed anything to call. I assured them I would.

I immediately called the hospice nurse who then told me there was a pill in the med kit for what Becky was going through. Seriously? Yes, there was a pill! This anxious feeling was something that happens with this cancer stuff and they have a med for that. I quickly got out our little med kit we had been given and we got that pill taken. It did seem to help, at least for a while. I called the nurse back and told her that something was changing with Becky. I explained how Becky's talking was not making sense to us. She said she would be coming over the morning and check on that. I wasn't comfortable with her answer, but I hung up the phone knowing I could always call back if things got worse.

It would be a long few hours for the two of us that evening. Becky would rest for a few minutes and then get up. She and I would go walking…again. She would talk about needing to do something or she would keep asking me if she had taken all her pills for the day. I did my best to talk to her while we walked around the house. She wasn't making any sense most of the time as we walked along. I was completely taken back by this new change because just the day before we had talked about all kinds of things with no problem. She had been tired before, but this was so different. I was trying to keep myself together, but I would have to turn away at times so she wouldn't see my eyes filling with tears. She was losing this battle and it was happening right in front of me. I was watching cancer take my wife away one minute at a time.

I never thought it was going to be like this.

I called the nurse later that evening on one of our strolls around the house. I was talking to her about what was happening with Becky and the nurse once again reassured me this was very common. She told me it sounded like I was doing a great job and to just let her know if anything else changes. Ugh!

After I hung up the phone Becky said in an almost childlike voice, "That lady could sure talk a lot."

"You mean the lady on the phone?" I asked.

"That lady could sure talk a lot." She was smiling, almost giggling like a little kid.

It really was like being with a small child. I wish I could write words that could express what I was feeling, but I can't find those words. It was an experience like no other I had ever gone through. We were in a new place. It was extremely emotionally draining, as you can imagine. Once again, there is no training manual for walking your wife around the house while cancer shuts down all of her systems. You just have to walk through that valley.

125

I finally got her back in bed and I thought maybe this time she would fall asleep. She could always sleep and I was convinced that if she could just calm down a little more everything would be fine until the morning. I walked out of the bedroom to get a little break from all the action because I was exhausted, but I could hear her again…talking.

I came walking back into the room and Becky was sitting at the edge of bed. Her first words to me were, "How old do you think that little girl is?"

"What little girl?" I asked.

"That one over there," she replied.

I'm telling you, I didn't want to look "over there." I'm smiling now as I write this part. I wasn't sure what she was seeing, but I was certain she was seeing something or in this case, someone. She asked again, "How old do you think she is?"

"I don't know…10, do you suppose?" I responded.

"Yes," she said, "10. Or maybe 7."

You might be wondering how I can recall all of this so well. Two reasons. One, you don't forget things like this… ever. Two, I made it a point to write it down afterwards so I could tell the girls. I was walking in a scary/amazing place. I knew that! I was trying to take it all in and at the same time stay focused on what I needed to do.

It was time to get to bed…again, but I noticed her PJs were wet. My emotional tank was getting empty and my mind was racing. "What is this now? What is going on?" I asked. It was then I realized the drain in her tummy was leaking.

Are you serious? Do we have to deal with this now? Should I be touching that liquid? Is that safe?

I had gotten that liquid all over my hands and of course it was all over the bed too. I couldn't believe it. What else can go wrong? Becky could tell I was getting very frustrated, and she very calmly in that childlike voice said to me, "You can do it, Clyde. One thing at a time. You can do it."

There was a longer pause and she said, "We can do it."

*We can do it? Becky, right now **we** can't do anything!*

I was out of gas! I called the nurse, and she came right over to help. She told me immediately that the liquid wouldn't harm me, but we needed to get that thing fixed. She could also tell something had changed with Becky. She gave Becky another med which seemed to calm things down a little and we got the leak taken care of. Becky just stayed in the bed calmly while we worked with tape and gauze to get the crazy thing functioning correctly. When we finished, the nurse said she would be back early in the morning.

The nurse left us there. I was a little more confident now for some reason, but then it hit me…the bedding was wet. I didn't know where the clean sheets were. I told Becky that we needed to get her up so I could change the sheets. She was very confused about this new order coming from me, and as I got her up to stand she got very concerned about things. Her voice cracked a little as she spoke, "What do you want me to do?"

I tried to explain, "I need you to sit over here in the chair, okay? I need to change the sheets because they are wet."

She was very worried now and almost crying, "What do I need to do?" she softly asked.

"Just sit here. Okay?" I said. I was trying to keep myself together. She sounded so sad.

She finally sat down on the chair next to the bed, but I could tell she was really concerned about everything and her worried whimpers were not helping my state of mind at all. I proceeded to vent out loud, not at her, but just to let out how frustrating it was that I didn't know where the sheets were kept. I'm sure my voice had a tinge of pain as well. This was really getting hard. Then, just like a switch had been thrown, her voice changed back into "normal Becky" and she said, "Clyde, those sheets are in the closet right there behind the door."

Just like that she was back. She proceeded to tell me where the sheets were and how to get the fitted sheet on the bed. She took me through the whole process step by step until I had my bedsheet project finished. I was told later, as I talked to medical people who explained what was happening, that her kidneys and liver were not working correctly and her mind was being poisoned. For a brief moment you might have a clear head followed by confusion. It all depended on the level of the poison in her system. That, of course is all very logical, but I want to believe God knew I needed a break. I'll let you all decide for yourselves on that one.

We had new sheets on the bed now.

I was so tired and so ready to get into bed and get some rest. I got her up out of the chair and put her in bed. It seemed like all was well. Time to sleep. My mind was racing. *What will tomorrow bring? We are going to have to do something about this tomorrow. What was that going to be?* I wasn't sure I could keep it up.

Jesus be near because this is really hard.

Then just like before, Becky was getting up again! I turned on the light, and there she was standing at the foot of the bed. With that frail little voice she spoke again, "I don't know what to do. I don't know what to do, Clyde...I don't know."

She was crying too, very softly.

"Go to bed, Becky." Now my voice was starting to crack. I was so out of gas.

"I don't know what to do," she said. "Clyde, why can't I think? I don't know what to do."

She would say it over and over while she stood there slowly rocking back and forth. I was nearly too tired to get up, but I knew I needed to get up and get a hold of her before the poor girl fell.

Then....

Her face changed. She stopped rocking and she stood tall. "Jesus knows what to do," she said. She smiled a little, "Jesus knows what to do."

She walked back to the bed, got in on her own, and pulled up the blankets. There was peace. The room was almost holy.

I have told this story dozens of times. I shared it at Becky's life celebration too. It has become a kind of theme around our church. The words that Becky spoke, "Jesus knows what to do" have become a powerful reminder of the presence of God in our lives. I told the girls the very next day about the whole episode and what their mom had said. They were not surprised. Jesus was always near to their mom.

I know there are many who would simply explain this all away as a reaction to the poisons moving around in her system, and maybe so, but somehow in some deep place in

Becky's mind she was able to draw strength from the One she had been trusting all along. He had been there for her again.

I turned off the lights and she and I slept the night away together...one last time.

I awoke the next morning and realized that she indeed had slept all night. She was still sleeping and resting very comfortably, so I got up and got ready for the day. I got her pills ready and waited for the nurse to arrive. Becky woke up and needed do the morning bathroom battle which went okay, but again, not the best. She was so tired and still a little confused. We did the pill thing, and I got her back in bed.

The doorbell rang and the nurse came in. She walked directly back into the bedroom and then returned to the kitchen where I was standing. She simply said, "It's time."

Becky and I had not talked about this, and I wondered how that conversation was going to go. I mean this was a big moment when you leave your house for the hospice house. It is more than just going on a little mini-vacation. You may never come back. I had been there for other people in these moments and I knew from experience what this was all about. The nurse assured me it might go better than I thought. So I gathered up my emotional self and walked back to the bedroom with the nurse.

Becky was in bed. Awake and resting comfortably. The nurse sat down next to her on the bed and said, "Becky, I think it would be good if we could go some place where we could take better care of you, and then your family won't have to do all this for you. Do you think we could do that?"

Without a second's hesitation Becky said, "I think that would be good."

I was stunned. Could it be that easy?

The landscape was changing so fast. Every hour it seemed.

....

It Was Time.

The nurse told me she had already called the hospice house on her way over to our house to make certain there was a room open. She said a room had just opened the evening before. Room number one. I am not kidding. Room number one. She said she would go get things ready for us and asked if I was okay with getting Becky ready to go. I assured her I could do that. Becky and I would get ready right away. After the nurse left I called Liz and told her what we were going to do. Of course Liz wanted to know if I wanted her, Abbie, and Dalton to come over and help. I told her I thought this was something her Mom and I needed to do alone. She understood.

I got a little bag of things ready and took it out to the car. I came back in and got Becky dressed for the short ride to her new home. We only lived a short distance from the hospice house, so the drive wouldn't take too long.

It was time to go.

Those are five little words, but there is lifetime's worth of thoughts going through your head. I don't know how to express it in words.

It was time to go.

I helped her sit up on the edge of the bed as I put the little flats with the fancy beads on her feet and stood her up. I thought she had herself under control, but she was weak now and not at all ready to stand on her own. She couldn't hold herself up. She lightly sat down on the bed. I reached down and carefully picked her up again. She stood there and looked at me. I mean looked at me. *This moment is one that I still can't get out of my mind.* I have never forgotten that look. I have told only a few people this part of the story, but I feel like I need to share it now.

She was "looking" at me for maybe 10 seconds. It was long enough to be a little…I can't find that word. We both just stood there. It was the moment in this long battle when I believe she was telling me with her eyes that she knew this was it. I could see it in her face. She wanted me to know. The words couldn't come for her, but her eyes were telling me what her tongue couldn't say. Only the eyes with a lifetime of memories can speak like that. I know this may sound a little over the top, but people, this was my wife who was dying of cancer. She had been at this for over a year and a half now. She had been through hell. We were sharing the end now, together. I was trying my best to keep myself together through all of this because I had to walk this girl out of our house…and there were stairs. I also didn't know if she was going leave without incident. Was she going to start crying? Was she going to start holding on to things? I needed to turn her attention to the matter at hand and get moving.

"Ok, Becky, here we go."

I was holding on to her because she was very weak. We walked out of the bedroom, down the hallway, past the kitchen to the stairs. There was a pause at the top of the stairs. She said, "I don't know if I can do it."

"We can do it together," I said.

And so, one step at a time, we went down...slowly....we made it to the landing. Then across the entry way and two more steps down to the garage. I put her in the car. We had made it! She never shed a single tear. She never looked around and never looked back. Inside I was a mess, but I had to keep going. The drive was not that far, as I explained earlier. While we were driving there, she gave me a little smile and made a little fun jab about my driving too fast.

You can't steal our joy!

I turned the last corner and drove to the front door of the Dougherty House. She was done, and I mean that. She couldn't get out of the car on her own power, so they brought a wheelchair and took her inside to room number one. We put her in the bed.

I know how painfully long this section of the book has been for you, but I wanted you all to read through these lines of memories in the hope that you might gain some perspective on what these tragic journeys are like. They are filled with so much emotion and so much sorrow, yet we were filled with such peace and comfort. Becky and her family were at this next new home and Jesus was there... waiting.

Chapter XI
The Final Days

The Dougherty House

The stay at the Dougherty House would prove to be much longer than we first thought. As events unfolded that first day, they told us Becky would not even make it through the night, but she would rally back later in the day. The first nurse in the room told me almost from the moment we arrived to settle in for a long journey…maybe seven days. My initial reaction was no way could that happen. I was wrong.

I am going to tell this part of the story by letting you read through the daily posts I put on social media. I decided there is just no way I could write it any better. The only thing I want to share with you before you read this next section is to share a word about the hospice people.

They are like angels who attend. I have never seen such compassion before in my life. Those "friends" have an amazing sense of just how much to do and how much not to do. They know what to expect in the situation and what you expect from them. I have nothing but complete respect for what they do. Our experience in that place was nothing short of wonderful. These times would be one of the most difficult paths our family will ever walk together, but these "attending angels" were so comforting in the midst of our pain. We loved those folks. They were there for us.

Here is Becky's hospice journey told through the daily posts as we waited for Jesus to take her home.

Day One
Me:

> *I'm going to write a short post this evening for Becky. We are now in Hospice care for her. We moved her today. Things have really gone downhill in the last 24 hours. She is a little confused…tired…pain free for the most part… life is precious. Thanks for the prayers everyone. Our long journey continues, but we are in a new day now.*

Day Two
Abbie:

I will give an update on Mom- Becky Teel: We are in the hospice house today. She and Dad checked in yesterday morning. Mom had a rough Sunday and just continued to deteriorate through Monday evening. On Tuesday morning the hospice nurse called Dad and told him there was a bed/room available if they wanted it. When Dad asked Mom, she was completely ready to go. So, here we are. Mom is resting comfortably pretty much all of the time. She is not able to talk to anyone, but she does know our voices. We are spending lots of time with just the five of us and that has been very good. The tears are right there as we look into the room and see Mom lying there. But we are all at peace through the sadness. We are thankful and humbled by all of the wonderful responses of support we have gotten throughout this journey. God is good and He is working all of this for His glory. We may not know what to do at times, but as Mom told Dad, "Jesus knows what to do." Yes He does, so we lean on Him. Blessings on you

Me:

Day two hospice care. Becky now…less words…only just a few things said…one word at a time. Still knows us. Can't take pills anymore. Morphine drip now…she is calm and resting.

*Some family stopped over to say goodbye.
Jesus be near.*

*We are doing fine. It's a sad thing though.
Peace still reigns and the angels are here.
Thanks everyone for the words. Powerful*

Day Three
Me:

Today was another day with our Becky. She is slowing down even more. Breathing so deep...but only just a few times each minute. We were told to prepare for a long wait. You just don't know how this will go they said. I think that was good advice. We are stilling our spirits and not looking ahead too far. That's a better place to do this. Oh the things we have to learn!

She doesn't talk to us now with her voice, but sometimes her eyes say so much. The distance between earth and heaven is closing. We long for her to go, but still hold on a bit...'cause that's what we all do. I told someone today that this new place is everything I thought it would be and yet in a way...nothing like I thought it would be. Maybe some of you will understand that...I suppose if you've been down this road.
Pray her home to Jesus friends...pray her home to Jesus.

Day Four
Me:

Becky is still doing what we were all created to do...living. Every healthy cell in us works to preserve the life it was given. It's how it was intended to be...now it's broken. She had a long day. Breathing so deep and so slow. You wonder how can she keep going? So...we decided rather than focus on the length of time and the struggle, let's focus on her amazing ability to hold on to her precious life with every ounce of energy she can find. We are after all...fearfully and wonderfully made.

It is changing though with each hour...we see it. The breathing now is different. Its depth not as strong...the end...we don't know how far yet the journey must go. We trust in One so much bigger than our frail ability to determine or comprehend. There is peace there.

Jesus hold Becky close. Let her see your face...soon.

Walk with her to a place you said you were preparing for her.
You know the way...because you are the Way.
Pray for the journey home.

Day Five
Me:

Becky holds on still. The morning started with her breathing comfortably. She was calm...peaceful. It was a gift for a few hours. Then things got a little bumpy. Pain... struggle...hard to watch. Will this be it? No...she rallied back again. We are amazed at this journey she is on. At times so peaceful and at other times a little rough. She got to say goodbye to the last sister who came today...that was an amazing moment when you think she's not taking much in...and she understood who that was...it was very obvious.

So now we wait some more. She is breathing deep again. That heart and those lungs are working...everything else they say has stopped. Yet she goes on. We wait for glory with her.

It is hard..very hard at times. Emotions are there...this has been a long road. Our peace and our strength is coming from a place we almost can't describe. It is a gift that only comes on the ground we now stand. It is holy.

Tomorrow is Sunday...she told me before this part came don't stop now...this is when it really matters. So I will be there. Go God Go!

Day Six
Me:

Becky is still with us. We did church this morning. That was Becky's request...always.
She is in God's hands...He is in control and we are at peace with that.
We wait.

135

Day Seven
Me:

> *Still waiting...weary.*
> *Quiet.*
> *Don't be afraid.*
> *Jesus come quickly.*

Day Eight
Me:

> *We have been so weary at times. This is just so long. She hasn't been responding to us for about 3 days now. We still go in and visit and talk, but what a journey. Last night we were all so worn down from it all. So...I said...let's all go home have a good cry and rest...she'll be here in the morning...and she was. Today is different.*
>
> *I think we are all beginning to understand some of why it is going so long. We understand the amazing creation of the body and how it can become so good at holding on to life. We also can see that we can't control any of this...we never did...that is in Another's hands. Becky is being fitted for heaven and we are being fitted for the next step in our lives. It's all a part of something far beyond what we can fully comprehend. There is rest in that place...we have discovered that.*
>
> *So friends...we wait for the next day...just like you...just like every life reading this word. Not really knowing what the next second may bring, but this family has the assurance that we are loved by a God who is holding Becky now even closer than even one moment ago. We feel that...believe that...trust that...live in that.*
>
> *Praying for a stillness in our spirit and the calmness in our hearts as we wait for all that is ahead.*

Abbie's Blog written that Tuesday evening for Wednesday:

Wednesday, May 28, 2014
Attuned To His Voice

Psalm 46:10 "Be still and know that I am God; I will be exalted among the nations, I will be exalted in the earth."

When we are still, we can actually see God moving. We are not distracted by our own flailing or by the flailing of others. We are able to intentionally focus on God and see His design in our lives. The other perk of being still is that there is a quietness that allows us to listen for His voice and discern what it is He is calling us to do. We can only become attuned to His voice when we hear it often, and He can only be heard in the stillness, so make time to be still with God. If you spend intentional time with God, keep your eyes and ears open because He will show up. We are experiencing this as a family in this time as we wait with Mom in hospice. We understand that we need to be still, and we have been able to see all that God has been doing in this time. He is being exalted!

Becky's In Heaven

Becky passed away early on a Wednesday morning. I had gone home like all the other nights before. The hospice journey had become a kind of routine now for us. I was only a short drive from there so if things started happening the nurses would call. I never worried about Becky being alone in that place. Becky and I had covered all that ground so many times before. We would talk very openly about all these things. I'm so glad we did. It was about 1:20am on that Wednesday morning. I was sleeping and was awakened by the ringing phone. I knew. I answered and this soft voice told me *Becky was gone.*

The nurse told me she had walked into the room to check on the pain med pump because she could hear the alarm going. It was the battery. Becky was still breathing away ever so softly. Her breathing by this time had a little moan at the end, which would just tug at your heart strings.

The nurse said she left the room and quickly went down to the nurse's station, grabbed a couple of batteries, and came back to fix the alarm. She said she put in the new batteries, reset the pump, and then realized Becky wasn't breathing anymore. She was surprised how peacefully she had gone.

I said we would all be down as soon as we could. I called the girls and they said they would meet me there in a few minutes. I drove down alone again…made the same corners…to the front door…up the walk and into room number one. The double doors were both swung open now. I have been at bedsides of people when they have passed. It can be a little shocking, if that's the right word, because the departed one can look very different. They lose color and it is all very different, but in that room, Becky looked like Becky. The girls said it too. She looked so happy. It was like you could just go over, wake her up, and take her home. Except now…she was *home*.

The long struggle was over for Becky. It was a time of sorrow like I have never experienced before. There were a few details at the Daugherty House to take of, but once that was done, the girls and I went home.

Day Nine
Me:

Becky is in heaven.

The long journey in this battle is finally over.
We are so thankful for the many words and shared stories through our days of waiting. It means so much to us.
We are sad…
But we are rejoicing…
Cancer did not win!
Peace still reigns.

It is an absolutely beautiful morning here today…we had rain with thunder and lightning last night as well…telling us that something was coming. What a fitting testament the closing of this chapter. There is more to do yet…that I know.

I'll write more later this evening, but for now just know how much we have been touched by the many words shared with us. You are all amazing people. God has been working throughout and we can see that in so many places...He's not done yet...nor are we!

Blessings to all of you.

Liz wrote:

Hi friends,
As many of you already know, my sweet Mom went to be with Jesus early this morning. It has been such an incredible journey. We have experienced God in ways that are hard to explain. It's incredibly beautiful. As we stood by her bedside in the wee hours of the morning and looked at her beautiful face, I was reminded of the verse from Revelation where God declares, "Behold, I make all things new..." Mom looked amazing just lying there with the most peaceful look on her face. Even though she is gone from this world, I know without a doubt that she is now fully alive with Christ, and I'm going to see her again! Hallelujah!

Thanks so much for ALL of the comments, thoughts, prayers, hugs, offers to help, just everything. We feel so loved! And I feel extremely proud to know that MY Mom touched so many so deeply!

We will celebrate her life next week. Visitation will be at our church on Tuesday, June 3rd from 5-9 pm with family present from 6-8. And her Celebration of Life service will be Wednesday, June 4 at 2:00 pm - Community Reformed Church - Sioux Falls, SD. The address there is 6800 E 41st Street in Sioux Falls.

I'm so thankful for this experience and I praise God for all He has done. His grace and power are overwhelming us! We have deep joy and peace amidst this sadness. It is unlike anything we've ever experienced. We are good, because God is so good.

Grace and peace to you, my friends. And as always, many thanks and much love to all of you!

When I arrived back home that evening the weight of this crazy journey begin to hit. It came like waves. At first, I sat alone just gathering my thoughts with a few tears and then floodgates opened. I remember not being able to stop crying and not really wanting to. I stood in the hallway letting the days of sorrow pour out. I told her out loud through my tears how sorry I was for not always being the best husband I could have been. Then I would recall all the good things and cry some more. Loudly at times and I didn't care. This was my time to let it all go. What a crazy ride this had been! There were so many ups and downs. She had gone through so much. I could feel the pain of watching. I had sadness for her struggle. That poor girl! The hours of tummy aches and the fever shivers. All of it now was too much for my weary heart to hold in and I was letting it go. I would eventually walk back to that bedroom and get some much-needed rest. I was at peace, but there was a penetrating sorrow. It was very real!

Chapter XII
The Life Celebration

Planning Becky's Day

The next day I called my funeral director friend Darin, who was going to be doing the arrangements, and we agreed to meet that morning to go over things for the funeral. I called the girls and gave them the information, and we met later that morning to talk about their mom's final day. Darin was a long-time friend and I had done a number of funerals with him. He was a face I knew. I also had him call on a former student of mine from back in Burke, Brian. Brian now was a funeral director in Beresford South Dakota, and I wanted him to help as well. We were going to take Becky back to Burke to be buried. That was home for us and we all thought that was the best for her and for us. The meeting went very well. I had done this kind of thing before, after all I am a pastor, so I knew what needed to be done. Becky didn't have any specific plans, only that she wanted *us* to do it all. We understood what that meant. Becky didn't have a favorite scripture or favorite song. That's not the way she was. It was all good in her eyes.

"You'll know what to sing," she would say. "You'll know what to say."

I knew what she meant. We wanted to do it right. Not make a big scene, but do it like she would want. The service is on the web at https://vimeo.com/98232945, if you would like to watch.

There were lots of calls yet to be made and plans of course, but none of that seemed to really be a bother to us. It was almost as though now we had something to do, so let's get busy. This is for Becky! One last time! Let's do this thing! We knew so many people had been watching and praying. Becky's story had touched hundreds of people, if not thousands. We knew people were going to ask, *"What does a preacher say when so many people were praying and yet this happened?"* There would be big questions as there always are. Why would God let this happen to this nice lady? Where was God in all of this?

We worked out all of the details and had everything ready to go. It was time to go see her.

I know from experience this is not easy for families. The first time you see someone in that place can be very painful.

We met Darin at the front door of the funeral home and he took us back to see Becky. As we walked along he was already apologizing because he was pretty sure he didn't get the hair right.

There was Becky. She had on her pink top. All the church folks probably remember that particular one. She was very into bright colors. I'm not sure where that came from, but it was her style. She looked just fine but, "The hair isn't right, Darin!"

You can't steal our joy!

We all set about the task of getting the hair *right*. This was our hairstylist for goodness sakes; we were going to fix that hair. He ran back and brought us a couple of brushes and we went to work on the hair until we got those bangs to poof just right. She looked amazing. She really did!

God, you did just fine! She was fitted for heaven.

That evening was the visitation. Earlier, in the late afternoon, the clouds rolled in and a soft rain begin to fall. It wasn't raining so much to keep people away, but just enough so you could hear the raindrops on the roof. We arrived at the church and set up some pictures and displays. It was the usual kinds of things families bring. We brought a few old things to bring back memories for us and for others.

There were flowers. There were flowers everywhere! I won't get into all that, but it was something to see. The guests started arriving. Remember this was a church of well over a thousand people and Sioux Falls is a close-knit community even though it's nearly 170,000 people. There are lots of connections. One by one they would pass by Becky. There were lots of tears and lots of hugs. I'm not a hugger, but I told my church family I would remove my "no hug" policy for two days.

It was amazing to be there.

Becky was loved by so many. You could feel it.

The next day the sun was shining. It was a perfect spring morning. It was amazing. People were noticing this too and talking about it. The night before and the gentle rain…today the sun was shining. We were going to take a trip into a place called "Resurrection." It was Becky's Life Celebration day.

The kids, that means Dalton too, and I sang at the beginning. That is not easy, but it needed to be done. I had my dear friend Randy do an opening for us. Then it was my turn. I did Becky's day for her. I did my best for her. My theme was built around the idea of living our lives in resurrection. I am a storyteller, as you have probably gleaned from the stories in this book, so I told them the story of Becky and me walking out of the house together. I told the story about her confusion and her words, "Jesus knows what to do."

I had a preaching professor in Seminary who had a little tag line he would use whenever the class would come across a good theme. He would say, "That'll preach!"

Yes, Doc, that'll preach!

"That'll preach!"

There were people sitting and standing everywhere that day. They had all come to hear the story. She had touched so many lives and her story is still doing that. We let the congregation sing at the end one big last hymn. It was really something to hear them. I wish you all could have been there. It was life changing! God was there! I have no more words to say about that day, only that it was one of the most amazing days of my life.

Afterward people stayed for a long time. We talked about so many things. We laughed a lot, cried sometimes, and yes, there were even times when we were giggling through tears. Our lives were full, even now. We would take a trip with her back to Burke to the place where we would lay her down for the last time. We would arrive there with our family gathered at the grave. Then, as in any small town in South Dakota, everyone went back downtown for a time to spend with folks around there. People had been so gracious. I love my hometown!

It was over now. The days of doctors appointments were finished. No more trips for chemo anymore. No more pain. No more struggle. Becky was in the place she had been created to be. She was finally Home. Jesus did know what to do!

Chapter XIII
Lessons Along The Way

The Purpose

In making the decision to write Becky's story, I wanted to not only tell the story of her journey, but also to bring a word of comfort to those who are either in the same battle or a similar one. I also wanted to share things I have learned from the perspective of a pastor going through this with her. I very often have people ask me questions about what to do for their friends who are going through hard times. It seems as though we become paralyzed by the situation because we create a list of duties we believe must be done. This is certainly not going to be an exhaustive list of the *dos* and *don'ts* for those in suffering, but I hope it sheds light on a subject that gets little attention. I hope it makes a difference.

Cancer and other long-term illnesses are some of the most difficult battles people will face in their lives. There are great resources out there, but typically we only get them when we are right in the middle of the mess. I wanted this to be a proactive approach. I wrote Becky's story as a way to bring attention to this very thing. I learned so much from it all and that's what I want to share. The journey doesn't make me an automatic expert, but I do believe it gives me a perspective that I wish to share.

I have changed much in my own ministry because of what I have learned in these last few years. Some of the lessons might be challenging to hear because we think we know what people need. Much of what *we* think people need/want to hear is misguided by our own fears and uncomfortableness in these tragic moments. My prayer is for this information to give each of you a better understanding of what your friends are going through in their dark days. I hope I might help you answer those hard questions many of us have when good people are faced with situations like Becky's. She said very often that she wasn't going through this for nothing, and she didn't. We have seen her message touch hundreds of lives. I hope it has already made a difference in your life as you have read her story.

Let's get started:

The Word "Gone"

When our family had finished all the final plans and our lives began to settle down, the first thing that began to rattle my life was just how permanent death was. I know that may sound a bit obvious, but I don't know if our minds and hearts can fully grasp the depth of what "gone" really is in those first moments after such a tragedy. I began to understand at a deeper level that Becky wasn't ever going to call again. She wasn't going to come home from work...ever. She wasn't just away with her sisters. She was gone. There are still times when I still can't believe she is not here. I see a picture or some little reminder and I'm struck once again with that reality. She is not with us anymore. She is gone. And gone is really gone.

I have seen the struggle in other families too. Those ongoing struggles drain us in ways that are hard to express in words. There is a time during the battle when we wish our loved one could just be done with the battle because it is so hard to watch them go through it all. This feeling is only natural and perfectly understandable, but when that moment finally does come it is a whole new day. Gone is really gone!

People have a way of weaving their daily lives into ours and at each of these intersecting points there are living reminders of just how much we have lost. Therefore, be aware of how much this is affecting your friends who have lost loved ones. Every day is different for them. Some days will be better than others, but they have lost someone. That feeling changes them!

What Do We Say?

I find this to be the most frequently asked question. It is an uncomfortable moment. It's not like we spend our days working in this kind of sad environment. It is all new and we are just not equipped. Yet we have this sense that *great words* will make all the difference to our suffering friend. I would acknowledge that great words can be helpful, but we might be putting a little too much stock the *value* of our words. **Silence** can be as effective as any word. My advice is simple, be real. If you can't think of anything to say then just say, "I don't know what to say. I'm sorry." Your honesty in the moment will speak volumes. This leads me to share one of my favorite stories after Becky passed.

I regularly go to a fitness center in Sioux Falls as it is just a part of my daily routine. The fitness staff was so nice to us during Becky's long road through cancer. Very shortly after Becky passed, I went to the fitness center to do what I do there. I was immediately met by many of the staff wanting to offer their heart felt sympathies for my loss. They were very genuine sharing their concern for they knew Becky and had been following this with us for months. Becky would often go there to get a massage or just relax for a few minutes. On this day the staff was gathered around me and there were tears and hugs as you can imagine, but there was one particular staff member there who was watching from a distance.

I have a wonderful friend there, Matt. Matt has Down Syndrome. He is a kind, loving young man who works there doing all kinds of chores for the fitness center. Matt and I hit it off right away because Matt was a pretty good weight lifter. There were even times when we worked out together. He is a wonderful person who is very social in engaging with everyone who comes there. On this day Matt was watching from a distance as he was doing his work at the fitness center. I went down to the locker room and got ready to go upstairs to do my typical afternoon workout. As I started up the stairs, Matt called my name and asked, "Why was everyone giving you hugs?"

"Well, Matt, my wife passed away," I said rather quietly.

"Really?" he said with a very concerned look on his face. He just stood there for a brief moment looking at me. I said something to him and he said something back, but I don't recall what was shared in that brief moment. I proceeded up the stairs to the workout area.

After I had finished my workout, I went downstairs and into the locker room. There was Matt putting the towels in their proper place, he does his job with absolute precision. As I walked past him, he asked me this question, "Clyde, are you sad?"

"Yes, Matt. I am sad," I replied.

"I'm sad too," he said, "but tomorrow will get better."

For the next several weeks when I saw Matt, which was a considerable number of times, his greeting to me was the same.

"Clyde, are you sad today?" he would ask.

"Yes, Matt, I'm sad today," I would reply.

Each time he would answer back in a soft voice, "I'm sad too, but tomorrow will get better."

How simple, yet so deeply effective! He was affirming my sorrow and still offering a word of hope. He was entering into my world, if only for a brief moment, but it worked. I knew he meant every word of it. He was spot on! I have shared this story a number of times trying to instruct others on how and what to say to their friends or family because it worked so well for me. I'm not suggesting we use those exact words, although I have used those exact words myself since then, but the **sentiment** he was sharing was perfect. Matt was a kind voice bringing a healing word to his friend in need. No seminary degree necessary, just one big heart. That'll preach!

Cures

I was surprised by how overwhelming this became for us all. I fully expected people to share their ideas about new cures coming out in the cancer world, but I was not prepared for the intensity to which it happened. At the beginning of the battle we were all very open to all of this input, but as the days passed, or in Becky's case, months passed, those *helpful* suggestions began to take on a less than comforting tone. I don't know if it was that our ears were getting tired of hearing, or if we were feeling a kind of unending pressure. All I know is it would finally get to the point of just wanting all that to end. It was too much! I want you to understand, I am not suggesting you should stop sharing all these potential cures, but try to be **sensible** and **sensitive** when you do.

We need to find a balance in all of this. If you can, try to imagine what this is like on the receiving end. What do you do when your friends provide you with 25 cures for cancer? Which one do you choose? You can't do all of them! Which one works? Do all of them work? And if they all work, then no one would ever die of cancer. However, that's not what we see at all.

This try the next "cure for cancer" became like a whole other battle we had to face. We didn't need one more battle. I know people meant well. I never questioned that, but folks our cancer friends only have so much *fight* in them. I hope these words give a new perspective on how very important it is to sometimes just be silent.

I would also recommend that when you come across an idea for some new cure that you do a little research yourself. You can get much valuable information about many of these things. You can do a little research for your friend and in this way you don't put all that responsibility on them! Do some reading. Do some checking on their behalf. That can be helpful.

And with that thought, let me share one more thing. There are "bad people" out there in cancer-land who use fear to prey on their victims. Cancer victims and their families will do almost anything, buy almost anything, and go almost any place when they are frightened. This kind of *fear* drives them to spend fortunes on cures that have no possibility of ever making a difference. I am most aware that these cures are promoted as the perfect answer to the problem, but you have to be wise in this crazy world of wolves. The internet is filled with all kinds of "doctors." It is a sad truth, but we are not living in a perfect place. **Wisdom** is a great gift you can offer!

Lastly, I would say use good common sense. Be prayerful in how you approach this. Your thoughts and opinions matter to your friends, but don't misuse that privilege. You need to allow room for your friend, who is hurting more than you can imagine, to say to you, "No, thank you." Remember, they are doing the best they can with all the information they have. They might be making a mistake, but they need to be given respectable room to make their own decision.

The Ministry of Presence

This was a phrase I learned while going to seminary. We had several classes on how to share with people who are going through tragic moments. We would sit in class and talk in great detail about what to say and what *not* to say. The focus of the class was to be aware of the other person's needs and not get lost in our own personal struggles. You learn to be there for *them*...not you.

You learn that just being there is often more important than our words. We have talked about this previously, but I thought I would elaborate on this important idea. When people are hurting they need you. They simply need to know they are not alone. This may sound like an easy way out, but it is not. Many of you might be thinking, "We are Christian people! We surely have something more to offer than just sit there with them, right?" Well, my friends, this may not be true. Our words, no matter how well intended, can get in the way of conveying what we are really wanting to share. I have had very *few* conversations with hurting people who can remember a single word I said, but they remembered I was *there*.

Becky had so many good friends around her throughout her long journey and I did as well. We had friends who were incredibly caring, and those were the ones who were just being themselves. They certainly shared words, but I can't recall them. What I do remember is they were there…close by. Very often I only needed to know they cared. It is amazing how it works.

There is an old story about a mom who was waiting for her young son to arrive home from school one afternoon. She was getting a bit concerned because he was late and that wasn't like him. When he finally arrived home, the worried mom, in her frustration, snapped at him, "Young man, where have you been?"

The little boy answered, "I was helping James with his bike because his wheel fell off and he crashed."

"His wheel fell off?" she asked "So, you helped him out?"

"I did," the son answered back.

"Young man what do you know about putting wheels back on bikes?" the mother asked.

"I didn't put the wheel back on Mom." the boy explained, **"I just sat down and cried with him for a bit."**

There you have it. Sometimes the best thing we can do is to sit down and cry with them. It is a good lesson to learn.

A Miraculous Healing

I believe in miracles. I have seen them with my own eyes. There have been moments when the only explanation for what happened was that God had done something in a circumstance that was completely beyond this world. I know there are people whose diseases have been cured by the moving of the Spirit in their lives. Jesus was a healer and to deny His healing is denying a significant part of who we believe Him to be.

However, He didn't heal everyone and that is a truth we have to wrestle with. There are many stories in Scripture of the blind seeing and the lame walking again, but we know there were scores of people He did not heal. This is not something we like to admit, but it is a reality that we must deal with. God does not always change the circumstance around us. The apostle Paul prayed three times for a "pain" in his life to be removed, and God didn't do it. Paul said that God's answer to his request was, "My grace is sufficient."

Here is another truth in life; we are all going to die. I often tell people we all have a "terminal condition." We are humans in a broken/fallen world. Death is a part of life on this side of Heaven.

It can be encouraging to hear the amazing stories of people who appeared to be dying of some illness and then everything changed...sometimes at the very last second. When everyone around them had given up, God did what only God can do. I love those stories and they can bring such hope and confidence. Becky and I noticed at the beginning of her journey those stories brought great encouragement, but the longer she went those same stories started to take on a new life. Those stories started to become somewhat painful to hear.

I remember one of Becky's friends was with her during the last few days of her life reading one healing story after another to her. I heard Becky stop her friend and tell her in a very nice way to stop reading those. Becky's words were, "Those stories are *their* stories, but maybe not mine." You might be questioning what Becky meant. Was she giving up? Was it Becky's way of saying, "Well sure that happens for others, but it can't happen for me."

When I asked her about that, she told me something I have not forgotten. Her words have changed my perspective greatly. She challenged me to **go deeper than an "outward" healing**. Becky said her cancer journey brought her just as close to God as those who had been outwardly healed. God was walking with her through this in a way that she had never known before. Together she and God were doing a work for the Kingdom. It wasn't about her. It was for others.

She had become that kind of person in this battle. You can talk to people who knew her well, and they will all tell you this is what she believed. God heals in many different ways and for many different reasons. Some of those reasons we may know and some we may not, but the greater purpose is trusting Him and walking close to Him. Jesus really is all you need. When He is all you have, you just might discover this kind of "healing."

She's in a better place.

This was a phrase I heard over and over after Becky passed. I have said it myself when those who have been suffering are finally in a place where all is well again. However, you don't have to tell a preacher that his Pentecostal-Jesus-loving wife is in a better place. That is a sermon *I don't* need.

Have I gotten your attention on this one? I hope so.

It never occurred to me that saying these words was not removing all the pain of loss as much as we might think. When I would hear people say, "She's in a better place." My heart would say, "I know she's in Heaven, but she's not *here* with *me.*"

I was missing Becky *here*, and knowing she was in Heaven was a wonderful and comforting truth, but no matter how deeply I believed she was there, this other truth was just as real. She is not here! I fully expect readers to think I'm being selfish, but let's go a little deeper.

The reason we all hurt when a loved one dies is because we feel a deep sense of loss. They are not here with us anymore. We can't talk to them. They don't come home anymore. Indeed, Heaven is an amazing place and I certainly wouldn't want to take her away from that new home, but I don't like the fact that she is not here. I had more things I wanted us to experience together. She is in Heaven and as comforting as that is, there is a part of me that is hurting because she is not with me. I wanted my friends to understand that.

I talk to people very differently now about Heaven and their loved ones who have gone on before them. I make sure I let those people know not only is their departed loved one in a wonderful place, but I want them to know I know it hurts. You need to say both things. That's the point I'm trying to make! I have visited with numbers of other people about this and all of them have told me the same thing about this very subject, so I know it's real.

Scripture

I am not going to share an exhaustive list of scriptures to use when people are suffering. I am going to share how Scripture talks about suffering.

Scripture talks often about suffering. You will find many texts in the Bible written around this subject. The Psalms are filled with wonderful words for people during hard times. As you read through them, you begin to see the words were often written during a difficult journey. God was on the journey with them. You will read entire sections where the psalmist is questioning all kinds of things. Where is God during this tragedy? The writers of the Psalms were not afraid to voice their impatience and, in many cases, even their disgust with God. I could offer any number of examples, but I would rather you go to the book and discover for yourself. By doing a little Bible study you may begin to find a whole new resource for sharing with your friends. The words will have meaning for you as well, and that becomes a wonderful message to share with a hurting friend.

Don't forget to bring *yourself* to your friend's side as well. Don't let Scripture take the place of *you*. Your hurting friend might want you to sit and say nothing. They may want *you* there more than any words you could ever share.

Prayer

Our family often wondered how many people had been praying for Becky. The number had to be overwhelming because we had lived in three different communities in our lives and had sung as family all over the Midwest. It had to be thousands of people praying. We received emails and cards from all over the country. Abbie had over 70,000 hits on her blog site in 2014. I am not sharing this number as a way of highlighting our popularity. Rather, I'm trying to make a point.

If that many people were praying, why wasn't Becky healed of her cancer?

I have had this very question posed to me several times *during* her journey and certainly after she passed even more. This question rattles our faith. Why didn't she live? What did we do wrong? I did get confronted by some who did say we must have done something wrong. That's a painful thing to hear! What I will offer here is more reflective than substantive.

I pray "vocationally" you might say. I have been at the bedsides of many very sick people and have offered up a word to God on their behalf. I never doubted each time I prayed that God *was* listening. Let me say it again. I have never doubted! He was far ahead of my words. He was working in that person's life long before my words were spoken. I know our prayers bring much comfort to people in tough times. Praying is the one thing we all can do for each other.

Yet, I meet people all the time who are confused by *how* they should pray. They wonder if they are using the right words or maybe wonder if God is listening to them because they have been "bad" that week. They ask God to do something and when they don't see His response they become confused or angry.

"Is it me?" they ask.
"Is it the words I am using?"
"Am I not trusting enough?"
"Is God angry at me?"

I have learned some things during this journey. I don't want to suggest for even a moment that I have mastered the art of prayer or that I have a complete understanding of every detail about the subject. I have been in a place where you are crying out to God and not seeing things happen. As a matter of fact, it seemed to be going in the wrong direction. What then?

"Did I pray incorrectly?"

When it comes to the right words I don't know how much they matter. I have to believe that prayer is so much more about **the heart** of the person praying and surely somewhat less about *what* they are saying. When children pray, do you suppose God turns a deaf ear to their limited choice of words, or do you think He listens? Of course, we know that answer. Jesus loved those little ones because of their innocence. I heard a speaker once talk about prayer. He said he thought God was not at all concerned with our words, but rather our heart-deep passion. He talked about praying as you run down the hallway towards your bedroom, falling to your knees sliding to the edge of your bed the whole time crying, "God!" That always made some very practical sense to me.

If God answers prayers when the right words spoken, then surely with the thousands of prayers being offered for Becky, one of those people would have been doing it "right." If it was about the perfect prayer, then surely one person out of that large contingency of prayer warriors would have had all the right pieces in place. But that is not what happened.

I believe God did answer our prayers. I now pray for the wisdom to see the answer.

"God, show me your vision!"
"Reveal Your heart to me in this struggle!"
"Open my eyes so that I can see your Glory!"
"Don't let me miss your Glory!"

Our family saw God's hand moving over and over again. We saw how He was using Becky and her story to bring change into people's lives. I saw how He was changing us for something that we at the time could not see, but we trusted was coming. I was praying to be surrendered to His plan and purpose.

"God, make me your instrument."
"I am yours."

Those prayers *were* being answered. We prayed for Becky to be healed. We prayed that the horrible disease she was fighting would go away. Thousands of people did. I believe God heard us! I have never doubted that! It hurts now and there is pain, but I have tried to live my life in a place where God is personal and not only doctrine. I seek God now to be a heart-deep sustaining power in my life. Prayer has become my way of connecting to Him who is already there. I'm praying to my Redeemer, for without Him I am lost.

I am writing these words not so you will be impressed by my faith. That is not the point. I want you to see the personal side of this. God wants us to be near him. It is what He desires most with us. Jesus died on the Cross of Calvary to close the distance between the Father in Heaven and the broken, wounded ones here on earth. Prayer then is not only my list of requests, but also drawing near to the most life-giving source I know. This leads me to the next point.

Prepare

We all get too busy with life. Our worlds become so cluttered we barely have time to get one task finished before the next one is presenting itself. "Busy" has become our god. Life passes by so quickly, and before you know it, your kids have grown up and the house is empty. It is another day, and then another. What happened to those last 10 years? Gone… and gone is gone.

However, what I want to talk about is not about good time management, but a different kind of **planning ahead**. We often think we can wait for the hard moment to arrive and then do something about it. We have this idea that we can wait to respond when the situation actually arrives. I want to caution you if are thinking that way. I believe Becky did so well through all of those rough days for a couple of reasons. First, because of the many prayers being offered up, she was being lifted up in a powerful way. Prayer was life-giving to her. But when I look back on her life, I want everyone to know a major reason for her strength came from her personal spiritual health. I hope that was evident as you read through her story. Her entire life was being sustained by something or should I say, *Someone* much greater than herself.

I can remember how uncomfortable she would get when people would tell her how they marveled at *her* strength. Becky would say over and over again,

"It's not me!"

She would tell folks that on her *own*, she was not a strong person. She was not the rugged, tough individual who could do great and mighty things. She would say her strength was all due to an amazing connection she had with God. Her deep connection to God had been nurtured long before there was a single cancer cell growing in her body. It was years of getting to know her Redeemer. It was going to Him when times were good. It was taking the time, no matter how full the plate, to foster this relationship. Then when the battle came, she was ready.

She did this through being a part of a healthy family, a spiritually healthy church, and her personal devotion to a loving God. **Spiritual health** can make all the difference in the world in times like this.

Fear

As I have grown older, death has taken on a new place in my heart. When we are younger death is not something we really give much thought to. I don't think it's always because we are afraid of it necessarily, I think it is mostly because we don't experience it the same way when we are young. Now I'm older and it is more real, but I fear it far less now than ever because of what I witnessed in this story.

I have told people that death is not so distant anymore. I don't mean in terms of time; I mean almost literally in distance. It is **one small step** away. I watched Becky go and what I saw was very tender. One moment she was here and in the next moment she was gone to another place. You could almost see it. I'm not trying to get all weird on you here. I am just saying death is certainly a part of this broken world. God is near during death and that journey is much shorter than we might think. There is nothing to fear when He is with us. I was deeply moved by that. Once again, I'm not offering a doctrinal word here about eternity. Rather, I'm offering a lesson taught to me by an experience.

I am not afraid.

Time doesn't heal all wounds.

I am starting to learn that I will carry a part of this journey with me for the rest of my life. I am not going to forget. As a matter of fact, I don't think I would like to forget. I can certainly move on, but I'm not going to forget. I will always carry a certain level of pain no matter how many days go by. The memories fade a little and the intensity of the hurt changes, but it is always at some level right there with us. There are moments, and they usually surprise me, when the pain is right there. Maybe a song, or a picture, maybe a moment, or maybe in the stillness of the day…you never forget.

Our lives are shaped by all these days we have lived. We have **transformational moments** that forever change us because of the intensity of the struggle. I believe this experience has prepared me for what is next. Some of that I have already seen and some of it I have not. It wasn't for nothing, of that I am sure. I go on with a confidence because I know God is ahead of me. I know it! I have some scars now, but they are reminders of a time when God was walking ahead of me, and Becky too. Time will not heal all of that; it can't. And because of what I have gained…I don't want to forget.

Chapter XIV
A New Orientation

Where was God?

What about God? Where was He? How could He let this happen? Why would He let this happen? Yes, why do things like this happen where such nice people have to go through such horrible things? These questions can haunt us for a lifetime. I want to offer an encouraging word at the end of "Becky's Journey" because after reading her story questions like those can take residence in your minds. My hope is that after reading her story you might be more *open* to listening. This is a deeply complex theological subject having been dealt with again and again in many books and writings. However, if this is keeping you from God or shaking the foundation of your faith, then you need to seek answers for your questions. If you are looking to argue or are simply unwilling to listen and learn, then nothing I can say will bring peace to your heart. That is a bridge only you can cross. I am going to offer a perspective that I hope you may find refreshing, but I know all too well there are no easy answers.

A New Orientation

I was given a book to read by a dear friend after Becky had passed as I was trying to decide what to do with Becky's story. The book was written by Walter Brueggemann. The book was entitled "Spirituality of the Psalms." I found the reading to be an uplifting voice in my journey. I was looking for something that could help give voice to what I was feeling. Brueggemann writes that our life's journey can be upset at times, *disoriented* if you will, and these seasons of distress have a deep purpose. It is during these times we discover God's sustaining presence at very new and profound levels. We may never experience them when life is "easy." Brueggemann would say, *"deep loss and amazing gifts are held together in powerful tension."*

Even people of faith may prefer to walk *around* the rough places. They avoid the paths of struggle as if there is nothing of value to be found in those footsteps, but there is *gain* in those rough places. There is a deepening of the soul to be discovered and a fresh hope of a promised new day.

Brueggemann calls this a "new orientation." God touches our hearts and brings us to a new land; a land flowing with milk and honey. The promised place we have been seeking. It is as if the struggle and pain have opened a door to a *new home* that God has built for us. Hope then returns and the glory of heaven comes to us once more.

I had witnessed this in my own life throughout Becky's battle. This final story is a grace-filled memory. It has increased my trust in God and His specific mercy focused on loving us *upward*. He is still able to reach down and bring life to us when all seems lost. I debated for a long time about putting this in the book, but I finally just gave in to what I felt was a pressing need to share this moment with you in the hopes that you will see how amazing God can be in the darkest of days. He never stops loving us!

One of Becky's concerns as she was losing her battle with cancer was how the disease was aging her. It is another battle to fight as you watch your body being worn away. Becky was not one to be consumed with externals as anyone who knew her well could testify, but for her this one last *challenge* was so discouraging. The hospice nurses told me that pancreatic cancer has a way of dramatically aging people. They told me I would watch my wife go from a middle-aged lady to an elderly woman in a matter of weeks. It is a sad truth about this awful disease and I could literally see it happening as the days passed.

Becky had a sister who had passed away a few years before. Her sister had colon cancer. The cancer had taken so much away from that poor girl that it was nearly impossible to recognize the once vibrant life that was lived. Cancer has a way of doing that. Becky said she was hoping she would not look that way when she died. She didn't want people to remember that image as the final picture of her life. She wanted people to remember "Becky" and not the person cancer had stolen. As the days passed, the reality of this happening to her seemed inevitable. The disease was robbing her of life on many levels.

Becky would often speak a little humor about how cancer was such a great weight loss program, but one she would not recommend. It was Becky's way of staying positive and joyful during this long struggle. She had lost over 70 pounds and she was slowly *fading* away a little more each day. As you can imagine, this kind of weight loss can leave a person looking extraordinarily thin and worn down. It seemed as though her concerns might come to pass. Was this disease going to take away her one last hope of looking like herself when she went home to be with Jesus? It wasn't as if we were completely fixated by this thought, but it was on her mind and something we all knew.

When she arrived at hospice that first day she looked so defeated, frail, weary, and for lack of a better way to describe it, she looked "old." Cancer had taken over her life. It had done what cancer can do. But as the days in hospice moved along we noticed a gradual *change* in that appearance. Her breathing was calm as you might expect from Becky. It was as though she was just in a new home resting peacefully. The girls and I would often tell her, "Becky, it's okay. You can go home now." There were times we would smile and say, "Becky go home now. You look just fine." It was all said and shared with great tenderness. It was our way of being conversational with her in these difficult moments. It was a way for our family deal with the sadness and pain during those final hours.

As the days passed it seemed to us that she...was looking better. Could that even be? Her skin seemed to be changing and her color was starting to look like *Becky*. It was amazing to witness. One afternoon the hospice nurse came in and started to fuss with Becky. I loved how the nurses would keep her lips moistened and put lotion on her hands and feet. They were so attentive to her needs. It was another of those gifts these hospice nurses could do for her. It was very special, a wonderful gift of care. So on this particular day the nurse was putting lotion on Becky's legs and I noticed a change there. I asked the nurse if she could see the change? The nurse of course wasn't sure what I meant so I explained. I told her when Becky had come in nearly a week ago there was lots of loose skin on her legs and arms from the tremendous weight loss, but now...it was all gone! The skin was no longer hanging. It was as if she was being *made new*. We started looking and noticed the small spots like bruises on her arms were almost gone and the skin on her neck was smooth again. Becky had changed!

Medical professionals would probably explain to us that because Becky had not eaten anything or had any fluids for several days that dehydration was causing a shrinking of the tissues. That might be, but it was a *miracle* for us. The nurses could see it too! Becky looked "new."

When she passed early that Wednesday morning her weight was nearly the same as the day we got married 40 years before. It was as if God had come and made His *bride* ready one last time. She had been fitted for Heaven. That earthly shell had been touched by the Maker's hand and the result was life-giving to us. Becky had gone to her new home, but God had granted mercy one last time. She would be the "beautiful pink angel" as one of the children from church described her on the day of Becky's life celebration. She looked just fine there in her pink outfit. God had shown up...even then!

It was a testament to God's walking with us through the darkest valleys and then bringing us to a new home...a new place. Our family had been changed by the journey and the God who walked with us through all those days had now brought about a visible change to our dear Becky. We had arrived at what Brueggemann would call a "new orientation." It became a sign to us of a peace and joy that not even cancer or death could steal. The grave did not win!

My life has been forever changed by this experience. Each step of the journey had its own set of obstacles and trials. I would find myself at times reeling from the next new challenge that was placed before me, and at the same time dealing with such sadness knowing Becky's struggle was so much greater than mine. I found myself feeling guilty for even thinking about my *own* pain. What kind of person takes time for their own pain when right next to them is someone dealing literally with life and death on a daily basis?

This conflict would never completely resolve itself and by the time I would start to get a handle on one part of the struggle something new would begin. I would find myself right back where I started reeling again. So this constant "disorientation" was so prevalent in my own story. I can't imagine how that was working with Becky. She never got a break! However, there were things being changed in me. There were things that needed to be deepened and broadened. There were perspectives to be discovered that have dramatically changed how I see the world and more importantly how I now share with others.

I now have a greater sense of my calling. I have a friend who shared with me that my *spiritual authority* has been elevated. My words have been given a new kind of strength. Experience is not only a great teacher, it also can be a great motivator for others. This "new orientation" is out there waiting for all of us as we move forward through this broken world. There is hope to be found in our honest pursuit of God's direction and purpose. We definitely can look ahead with a sense of *expectancy* that God is going to fill these empty vessels. If it worked in Becky's journey, then it can work for us as well.

God can be trusted. He is reliable. He who watches over us does not slumber. There will be a day when the flowers will bloom in the desert. The streams will flow once again and the rain will fall on the parched earth. I want you to know that the tears on this journey were all so real. The fear and the pain were so deep. I don't want to have to go through that again, nor would I wish it on anyone, but *I know that my Redeemer lives, and at the last he will stand upon the* earth. God was there through all Becky's days. He never left her side. He will never forsake us!

Jesus knows what to do.